UNLOCKING YOUR INNER STRENGTH

A GUIDE TO SELF-DISCOVERY AND PERSONAL GROWTH

BY

MUJAHID BAKHT

EBook ISBN: E- 979-8-9880391-9-8

Published by

Atlas Amazon, LLC

United States of America

TABLE OF CONTENTS

ABOUT AUTHER

LIFE HISTORY Mr. Bakht is a mature, experienced, extremely enthusiastic, energetic, administrator, and thirty-six years have proven experience as a businessman in international marketing and public relations. Mr. Bakht is an International Real Estate Specialist, and Professional Business and Projects Consultant. He was born in Pakistan, Educated in Pakistan and USA. Presently American Citizen belongs to a business-oriented family. Thirty-Six years Resident of New York, USA.

BUSINESS HISTORY: Mr. Bakht is a Founder & President of Atlas Amazon, LLC., Mr. Bakht is a business developer and multilingual business specialist in the Caribbean, South East Asia, and the Middle East emerging markets Mr. Bakht has served, met, and host many heads of the States. Also, maintain a close relationship with investors of high net worth in the USA.

CAREER: Mr. Bakht has been engaged with many multinational companies in the field of international real estate investment, communication, technology, diamond, gold, mining, Pre-Feb housing, wind & solar energy, outsourcing management, and project consulting along with business partners & associates worldwide. Mr. Bakht has participated in major national and international conferences including participated in United Nations (U.N.O.) conferences.

TRAVEL: Mr. Bakht is well-traveled and has visited many countries worldwide.

MANAGEMENT EXPERIENCE: Thirty-Six years of diversified experience in project consulting, marketing, and business management. As a Director of Marketing, Director of Public Relations, Director of International Affairs, Executive Vice President, President, CEO, and Chairman of many national & multinational companies. Mr. Bakht hired and trained many professionals as business consultants in international marketing and supervised them.

CERTIFICATE OF ACHIEVEMENT: Achievement Award was presented to Mr. Bakht by Stephen Fossler for five years of continued growth and customer satisfaction from 1996-to 2001.

HONORS MEMBER: Madison Who's Who of Professionals, having demonstrated exemplary achievement and distinguished contributions to the business community, registered at the Library of Congress in Washington D.C. USA. (2007 & 2008)

HONORS MEMBER: Premiere who's Who International, professional business executive having demonstrated exemplary achievement and distinguished contributions to the International business community, 2008 and 2009.

CERTIFICATES: Certificate of Authenticity from Bill Rodham Clinton, President of the United States, and Hillary Rodham Clinton First Lady, USA. (July 20, 2000);

CERTIFICATE OF AUTHENTICITY: from Terence R. McAuliffe, Chairman of Democratic National Committee, Tom Dachle, Senate Democratic Leader, Dick Gephardt, House Democratic Leader, USA. (June 16, 2001);

CERTIFICATE OF AUTHENTICITY: from Terence R. McAuliffe, Chairman of Democratic National Committee, USA. (April 16, 2002).

Chapter 1

INTRODUCTION

Unlocking inner strength is the process of discovering and utilizing one's inner resources and abilities to overcome challenges, achieve goals, and live a fulfilling life. It involves developing mental, emotional, and spiritual resilience that enables one to cope with adversity and harness their potential to reach their full potential.

Inner strength refers to the innate abilities that reside within every individual, such as willpower, courage, determination, self-discipline, and self-confidence. These qualities help individuals to withstand difficult situations and overcome obstacles, allowing them to achieve their goals and live a happy and fulfilling life. However, many individuals fail to recognize or develop these qualities, leading to self-doubt, low self-esteem, and a lack of motivation.

Unlocking inner strength begins with recognizing and accepting one's strengths and weaknesses. It involves self-reflection, self-awareness, and a willingness to change and grow. This process may be challenging, as it requires individuals to confront their fears, doubts, and negative beliefs, but it is essential for personal growth and development.

To unlock inner strength, individuals must develop a growth mindset, which is a belief that their abilities and intelligence can be developed through hard work and dedication. This mindset allows individuals to view challenges and setbacks as opportunities for growth and learning, rather than as obstacles to be avoided.

Inner strength also involves developing resilience, which is the ability to bounce back from adversity and maintain a positive outlook despite challenges. Resilience can be developed through various techniques, such as mindfulness, positive self-talk, and social support.

In addition, unlocking inner strength requires individuals to cultivate self-love and self-compassion. This involves treating oneself with kindness, understanding, and forgiveness, rather than self-criticism and judgement. It also involves setting healthy boundaries, prioritizing self-care, and practicing gratitude.

By unlocking their inner strength, individuals can improve their mental and emotional well-being, achieve their goals, and lead a more fulfilling life. They become more resilient, confident, and self-reliant, enabling them to overcome challenges and seize opportunities. They also develop stronger relationships, as they are better equipped to communicate their needs and feelings and understand those of others.

Overall, unlocking inner strength is a lifelong process of self-discovery and personal growth. It requires individuals to develop a growth mindset, cultivate resilience and self-love, and embrace challenges as opportunities for growth. By doing so, individuals can unlock their full potential and live a happy and fulfilling life.

The importance of self-discovery and personal growth

Self-discovery and personal growth are essential for individuals to live a fulfilling and meaningful life. These processes involve exploring one's values, beliefs, strengths, and weaknesses, and using this knowledge to make positive changes in one's life. The following are some of the reasons why self-discovery and personal growth are important:

Increased self-awareness: Self-discovery allows individuals to gain a better understanding of themselves, including their strengths, weaknesses, values, and beliefs. This knowledge enables individuals to make better decisions, set realistic goals, and live a more authentic life.

Improved mental and emotional well-being: Personal growth helps individuals to develop coping mechanisms, reduce stress and anxiety, and improve their overall mental and emotional well-being. This process involves cultivating positive emotions, such as gratitude, empathy, and compassion, and learning to manage negative emotions, such as fear and anger.

Greater sense of purpose: Self-discovery and personal growth help individuals to find their passion and purpose in life. This process involves exploring one's interests and values, and identifying activities that bring a sense of meaning and fulfillment. Having a clear sense of purpose can improve one's overall quality of life and provide a sense of direction.

Improved relationships: Personal growth involves improving communication skills, developing empathy and compassion, and setting healthy boundaries. These skills are essential for building and maintaining strong relationships with family, friends, and coworkers.

Increased resilience: Self-discovery and personal growth help individuals to develop resilience, which is the ability to bounce back from adversity and maintain a positive outlook despite challenges. Resilience enables individuals to cope with stress and setbacks and recover more quickly from difficult situations.

Enhanced creativity: Personal growth involves exploring new ideas and perspectives, which can enhance creativity and innovation. This process involves stepping outside of one's comfort zone, taking risks, and embracing new experiences.

Improved self-confidence: Self-discovery and personal growth help individuals to build self-confidence and self-esteem. This process involves setting goals, overcoming obstacles, and celebrating achievements, which can improve one's sense of self-worth.

Increased success: Personal growth is often associated with increased success in various aspects of life, including career, relationships, and personal goals. This process involves developing skills and habits that lead to success, such as discipline, persistence, and adaptability.

Self-discovery and personal growth are essential for individuals to live a fulfilling and meaningful life. These processes involve exploring one's values, beliefs, strengths, and weaknesses, and using this knowledge to make positive changes in one's life. By engaging in self-discovery and personal growth, individuals can improve their mental and emotional well-being, find their purpose in life, improve relationships, develop resilience, enhance creativity, build self-confidence, and increase success.

Chapter 2

UNDERSTANDING INNER STRENGTH

Inner strength refers to a person's ability to draw on their inner resources, such as mental and emotional resilience, in order to overcome difficult or challenging situations. It is the capacity to navigate life's obstacles with confidence, determination, and a sense of purpose. Inner strength is not an inherent trait, but rather a quality that can be cultivated through intentional practices and a growth mindset.

There are several key components of inner strength

Resilience - The ability to bounce back from setbacks, adapt to change, and overcome challenges.

Self-awareness - The ability to understand and manage one's emotions, thoughts, and behaviors.

Self-confidence - The belief in oneself and one's abilities.

Purpose - A sense of direction and meaning in life.

Emotional intelligence - The ability to recognize and manage one's own emotions and those of others.

Self-care - Prioritizing one's physical, emotional, and mental health.

Positive mindset - Focusing on the positive aspects of life and reframing negative experiences.

Inner strength is not a fixed trait that is present in some people and absent in others. Rather, it is a quality that can be developed through intentional practices and a growth mindset. Developing inner strength involves a willingness to confront one's fears and weaknesses, as well as a commitment to personal growth and self-improvement.

One way to cultivate inner strength is through self-reflection and self-awareness. By taking the time to reflect on one's thoughts, feelings, and behaviors, a person can gain a better understanding of their strengths and weaknesses, as well as their values and priorities. This can help them develop a sense of purpose and direction in life, and build resilience in the face of challenges.

Another way to cultivate inner strength is through building a support system of positive relationships. Having people in your life who believe in you, support you, and challenge you to grow can help you develop the resilience and self-confidence needed to overcome challenges and achieve your goals.

Developing inner strength also involves cultivating a growth mindset. This means seeing challenges and setbacks as opportunities for growth and learning, rather than as insurmountable obstacles. A growth mindset involves embracing change, taking risks, and seeking out new experiences and challenges.

Finally, developing inner strength involves prioritizing self-care. This means taking care of your physical, emotional, and mental health by getting enough rest, exercise, and healthy food, as well as seeking out support when needed. When we prioritize self-care, we are better equipped to handle life's challenges and maintain our inner strength.

Inner strength is a quality that can be cultivated through intentional practices and a growth mindset. By developing resilience, self-awareness, self-confidence, purpose, emotional intelligence, self-care, and a positive mindset, we can overcome life's challenges and achieve our goals with confidence and determination.

Different types of inner strength

Inner strength is a multifaceted concept, encompassing a range of different qualities and abilities that allow individuals to navigate life's challenges with resilience, courage, and determination. Here are some of the different types of inner strength:

Emotional resilience - Emotional resilience refers to the ability to bounce back from difficult emotions, such as sadness, anxiety, or disappointment. It involves the capacity to regulate one's own emotions, to express them effectively, and to cope with stressful

16

situations. Emotional resilience can be developed through practices such as mindfulness, meditation, and cognitive-behavioral therapy.

Mental toughness - Mental toughness is the ability to persist in the face of adversity and to maintain focus and determination in the pursuit of one's goals. It involves the capacity to remain calm and composed under pressure, to overcome self-doubt and negative self-talk, and to maintain a positive mindset even in challenging circumstances. Mental toughness can be developed through practices such as visualization, positive self-talk, and exposure therapy.

Physical resilience - Physical resilience refers to the ability to recover from physical challenges such as illness, injury, or trauma. It involves the capacity to maintain good health, to overcome physical obstacles, and to adapt to changes in one's body or environment. Physical resilience can be developed through practices such as exercise, proper nutrition, and stress management.

Spiritual strength - Spiritual strength refers to the ability to find meaning and purpose in life, and to connect with a higher power or a greater sense of purpose. It involves the capacity to transcend one's own ego and to see the bigger picture of life's challenges and opportunities. Spiritual strength can be developed through practices such as prayer, meditation, or community service.

Social resilience - Social resilience refers to the ability to maintain healthy relationships with others, even in the face of conflict or adversity. It involves the capacity to communicate effectively, to resolve conflicts constructively, and to seek out support when needed. Social resilience can be developed through practices such as active listening, assertiveness training, and group therapy.

Intellectual strength - Intellectual strength refers to the ability to think critically, to solve problems creatively, and to learn new things throughout life. It involves the capacity to process complex information, to analyze data, and to make informed decisions based on evidence and reason. Intellectual strength can be developed through practices such as reading, writing, and engaging in intellectually stimulating activities.

Creative strength - Creative strength refers to the ability to generate new ideas, to express oneself creatively, and to approach challenges with a sense of imagination and innovation. It involves the capacity to think outside the box, to take risks, and to experiment with new ways of doing things. Creative strength can be developed through practices such as art, music, or creative writing.

Moral strength - Moral strength refers to the ability to act in accordance with one's own values and principles, even in the face of opposition or temptation. It involves the capacity to make ethical decisions, to stand up for what one believes in, and to act with integrity and courage. Moral strength can be developed through practices such as ethical reflection, moral reasoning, and character education.

Inner strength is a complex and multifaceted concept that encompasses a range of different qualities and abilities. Emotional resilience, mental toughness, physical resilience, spiritual strength, social resilience, intellectual strength, creative strength, and moral strength are all important aspects of inner strength that can be developed through intentional practices and a growth mindset. By cultivating these different types of inner strength, individuals can overcome life's challenges with courage, resilience, and determination.

Benefits of having inner strength

Inner strength is essential for navigating life's challenges with resilience and determination. Here are some of the key benefits of having inner strength:

Improved mental health: Inner strength helps individuals to cope with stress and anxiety, which can have a positive impact on their mental health. When individuals have emotional resilience and mental toughness, they are better able to manage their emotions, maintain a positive outlook, and persevere in the face of adversity. This can help to reduce symptoms of depression and anxiety and improve overall mental wellbeing.

Greater self-awareness: When individuals develop their inner strength, they gain a greater sense of self-awareness and insight into their own thoughts, feelings, and behaviors. This can help them to identify areas for growth and development, and to work towards personal goals with greater clarity and purpose.

Increased confidence: Inner strength gives individuals the confidence to tackle new challenges and take risks. When individuals have the emotional resilience, mental toughness, and moral strength to persevere in the face of adversity, they are more likely to take on new challenges and pursue their goals with confidence and determination.

Improved relationships: When individuals have social resilience and moral strength, they are better able to maintain healthy relationships with others. They are able to communicate effectively, resolve conflicts constructively, and seek out support when needed. This can help to build stronger, more positive relationships with family, friends, and colleagues.

Better physical health: Inner strength can also have a positive impact on physical health. When individuals have physical resilience, they are better able to recover from illness or injury and maintain good health overall. When individuals have spiritual strength, they may be more likely to engage in healthy behaviors such as exercise, proper nutrition, and stress management.

Enhanced creativity: Inner strength can also enhance creativity. When individuals have creative strength, they are better able to approach problems with a sense of innovation and imagination, and to come up with new and original ideas. This can be beneficial in a range of contexts, from work and personal life to hobbies and artistic pursuits.

Increased resilience: Inner strength helps individuals to bounce back from setbacks and overcome obstacles. When individuals have emotional resilience, mental toughness, physical resilience, and social resilience, they are better able to navigate life's challenges with courage and determination.

Greater sense of purpose: Inner strength can also give individuals a greater sense of purpose and meaning in life. When individuals have spiritual strength, they may be more likely to feel connected to something larger than themselves and to find meaning in their experiences. This can help to cultivate a sense of purpose and direction in life.

having inner strength can bring a range of benefits, including improved mental health, greater self-awareness, increased confidence, improved relationships, better physical health, enhanced creativity, increased resilience, and a greater sense of purpose. By developing their emotional resilience, mental toughness, physical resilience, spiritual strength, social resilience, intellectual strength, creative strength, and moral strength, individuals can navigate life's challenges with resilience and determination, and cultivate a sense of wellbeing, purpose, and fulfillment in their lives.

Chapter 3

OVERCOMING SELF-DOUBT

Self-doubt is a common experience that can prevent individuals from realizing their full potential. It can cause individuals to feel unsure of themselves, their abilities, and their worth, and can prevent them from taking risks and pursuing their goals. Here are some common causes of self-doubt:

Past experiences: Past experiences can have a significant impact on an individual's sense of self-worth and self-confidence. Negative experiences, such as failures, rejection, or criticism, can lead individuals to doubt their abilities and worth. These experiences can create a negative self-image that can be difficult to overcome.

Comparisons to others: Comparing one to others can be a major cause of self-doubt. When individuals compare themselves to others, they may feel that they don't measure up, or that they are not as capable or successful as their peers. This can create feelings of inadequacy and undermine self-confidence.

Unrealistic expectations: Setting unrealistic expectations for oneself can also lead to self-doubt. When individuals set goals that are too high or expect perfection from themselves, they are more likely to feel like they have failed or fallen short of their expectations. This can undermine their sense of self-worth and lead to self-doubt.

Lack of experience: When individuals lack experience in a particular area, they may feel unsure of their abilities and unsure of how to proceed. This can lead to self-doubt and prevent them from pursuing new opportunities or taking risks.

Fear of failure: Fear of failure can be a major cause of self-doubt. When individuals are afraid of failing, they may be hesitant to take risks or pursue their goals, for fear of not measuring up or being seen as a failure. This fear can undermine their self-confidence and prevent them from realizing their full potential.

Negative self-talk: Negative self-talk, or the inner voice that criticizes and doubts oneself, can be a major cause of self-doubt. When individuals engage in negative self-talk, they may reinforce their own insecurities and doubts, and undermine their self-confidence.

Perfectionism: Perfectionism can also be a cause of self-doubt. When individuals strive for perfection, they may set unrealistic expectations for themselves and become overly critical of their own efforts. This can lead to feelings of inadequacy and undermine self-confidence.

External validation: Relying too much on external validation can also lead to self-doubt. When individuals rely on others to validate their worth or abilities, they may become overly dependent on external sources of approval and feel unsure of themselves when that validation is not present.

Self-doubt can be caused by a variety of factors, including past experiences, comparisons to others, unrealistic expectations, lack of experience, fear of failure, negative self-talk, perfectionism, and external validation. By understanding these causes, individuals can begin to identify and address the root causes of their self-doubt, and work towards building greater self-confidence and self-belief.

Strategies to overcome self-doubt

Self-doubt can be a difficult challenge to overcome, but there are many strategies that individuals can use to build greater self-confidence and overcome their insecurities. Here are some strategies for overcoming self-doubt:

Recognize and challenge negative self-talk: Negative self-talk can reinforce feelings of self-doubt and undermine self-confidence. To overcome this, individuals can begin by recognizing their negative self-talk and actively challenging it. For example, if an individual finds themselves thinking "I'm not good enough," they can challenge this thought by asking themselves "What evidence do I have to support this thought? Is this thought helpful or harmful to me?"

Set realistic goals: Setting realistic goals can help individuals to build confidence and avoid feelings of inadequacy or failure. By breaking larger goals into smaller, more achievable steps, individuals can build momentum and confidence as they work towards their larger goals.

Focus on strengths: Focusing on strengths rather than weaknesses can also help individuals to build confidence and overcome self-doubt. By identifying their strengths and using them to their advantage, individuals can feel more competent and capable, and can avoid focusing on their areas of weakness.

Take action: Taking action, even in the face of self-doubt, can be an effective way to build confidence and overcome insecurity. By taking small steps towards their goals, individuals can build momentum and confidence, and can gain a sense of accomplishment that can help to reinforce their self-belief.

Seek support: Seeking support from others can also be a powerful strategy for overcoming self-doubt. This might involve talking to a trusted friend or family member, or seeking support from a therapist or coach. By sharing their thoughts and feelings with others, individuals can gain perspective and support, and can build confidence through positive feedback and encouragement.

Practice self-care: Taking care of oneself can also be an important strategy for overcoming self-doubt. This might involve practicing relaxation techniques such as meditation or yoga, engaging in physical exercise, or getting enough sleep and nutrition. By taking care of their physical and emotional well-being, individuals can feel more confident and capable in their daily lives.

Learn from mistakes: Making mistakes is a normal part of the learning process, and can be an important opportunity for growth and self-improvement. By embracing mistakes and learning from them, individuals can build resilience and self-confidence, and can avoid becoming paralyzed by fear of failure.

Cultivate a growth mindset: Finally, cultivating a growth mindset can be a powerful strategy for overcoming self-doubt. A growth mindset involves viewing challenges and obstacles as opportunities for growth and learning, rather than as threats to one's self-worth. By adopting this mindset, individuals can build resilience and self-confidence, and can avoid becoming trapped in self-doubt.

Overcoming self-doubt is a complex and ongoing process, but there are many strategies that individuals can use to build greater self-confidence and overcome their insecurities. By challenging negative self-talk, setting realistic goals, focusing on strengths, taking action, seeking support, practicing self-care, learning from mistakes, and cultivating a growth mindset, individuals can build the resilience and self-belief they need to achieve their goals and live fulfilling lives.

The importance of self-compassion in overcoming self-doubt

Self-doubt can be a challenging experience that can negatively impact an individual's self-esteem, confidence, and overall well-being. While there are many strategies that individuals can use to overcome self-doubt, one particularly important approach is to practice self-compassion. Self-compassion involves treating oneself with kindness, understanding, and empathy, rather than self-criticism or self-judgment.

There are several reasons why self-compassion is important for overcoming self-doubt:

Self-compassion reduces self-criticism: When individuals experience self-doubt, they may be quick to criticize themselves for their perceived failures or shortcomings. This self-criticism can be particularly harsh, leading to feelings of shame, guilt, and inadequacy. However, by practicing self-compassion, individuals can learn to treat themselves with kindness and understanding, which can help to reduce self-criticism and promote self-acceptance.

Self-compassion fosters resilience: Self-compassion can also help individuals to build resilience in the face of challenges and setbacks. When individuals are able to treat themselves with kindness and empathy, they may be more likely to bounce back from failures or disappointments, and to view these experiences as opportunities for growth and learning.

Self-compassion promotes self-care: Practicing self-compassion can also encourage individuals to take care of their physical and emotional well-being. When individuals are able to treat themselves with kindness and understanding, they may be more likely to engage in activities that promote their health and well-being, such as exercising, eating well, and getting enough sleep.

Self-compassion improves relationships: Finally, practicing self-compassion can improve an individual's relationships with others. When individuals are able to treat themselves with kindness and empathy, they may be more likely to extend the same level of care and understanding to others, which can foster stronger and more fulfilling relationships.

So how can individuals practice self-compassion in the face of self-doubt? Here are some strategies:

Treat one as one would treat a friend: When individuals experience self-doubt, they may be quick to criticize themselves or engage in negative self-talk. To counteract this, individuals can try treating themselves as they would treat a close friend who is going through a difficult time. This might involve offering words of encouragement, expressing empathy, or engaging in acts of self-care.

Practice mindfulness: Mindfulness involves being present in the moment, without judgment or distraction. When individuals practice mindfulness, they can become more aware of their thoughts and feelings, and can learn to observe these experiences without becoming overwhelmed by them. This can help to reduce self-criticism and promote self-compassion.

Practice self-acceptance: Self-acceptance involves recognizing and accepting one's strengths and weaknesses, without judgment or criticism. When individuals practice self-acceptance, they can learn to treat themselves with kindness and understanding, even when they make mistakes or fall short of their goals.

Cultivate gratitude: Gratitude involves recognizing and appreciating the positive aspects of one's life, even in the face of challenges and difficulties. When individuals cultivate gratitude, they can learn to focus on the good in their lives, which can promote feelings of positivity and self-compassion.

Self-doubt can be a challenging experience, but practicing self-compassion can be a powerful tool for overcoming it. By treating oneself with kindness, empathy, and understanding, individuals can reduce self-criticism, foster resilience, promote self-care, and improve relationships. Strategies for practicing self-compassion might include treating oneself as one would treat a friend, practicing mindfulness, practicing self-acceptance, and cultivating gratitude. With time and

Chapter 4

DEVELOPING A GROWTH MINDSET

A growth mindset is a way of thinking and approaching life that is focused on growth, learning, and development. People with a growth mindset believe that their abilities and talents can be developed through hard work, effort, and perseverance, rather than being fixed or predetermined. This belief can lead to a more positive and productive approach to life, as individuals with a growth mindset are more likely to take on challenges, persist in the face of obstacles, and embrace opportunities for growth and learning.

The concept of a growth mindset was first introduced by psychologist Carol Dweck in her book, *"Mindset: The New Psychology of Success"*. Dweck's research suggests that individuals who have a growth mindset are more likely to achieve success in a variety of areas, including academics, athletics, and personal relationships.

At the core of the growth mindset is the belief that abilities and talents are not fixed traits, but rather can be developed and improved over time. This belief is in contrast to a fixed mindset, which suggests that abilities and talents are innate and cannot be changed or improved. People with a fixed mindset tend to focus on proving themselves and avoiding failure, whereas people with a growth mindset tend to focus on learning and improving.

Some key characteristics of a growth mindset include:

Embracing challenges: People with a growth mindset tend to see challenges as opportunities for growth and learning, rather than obstacles to be avoided. They are more likely to take on challenges and persist in the face of setbacks, as they see these experiences as opportunities to develop their abilities and skills.

Viewing failure as a learning opportunity: People with a growth mindset tend to view failure as a natural part of the learning process, rather than as a reflection of their abilities or worth as a person. They are more likely to learn from their mistakes and use these experiences to improve their performance in the future.

Valuing effort and perseverance: People with a growth mindset believe that hard work, effort, and perseverance are essential for achieving success. They are more likely to put in the necessary time and effort to achieve their goals, even when the path to success is difficult or uncertain.

Seeking out feedback and learning opportunities: People with a growth mindset are open to feedback and seek out opportunities for learning and development. They are more likely to seek feedback from others, ask questions, and engage in self-reflection to identify areas for improvement.

There are many benefits to having a growth mindset. Some of these benefits include:

Improved performance: People with a growth mindset are more likely to achieve success in a variety of areas, including academics, athletics, and personal relationships. By focusing on learning and improvement, rather than avoiding failure, they are more likely to take on challenges and persist in the face of setbacks, leading to improved performance over time.

Increased resilience: People with a growth mindset are more resilient in the face of adversity. They are better able to bounce back from setbacks and failures, as they see these experiences as opportunities for growth and learning.

Greater self-awareness: People with a growth mindset are more likely to engage in self-reflection and seek feedback from others. This can lead to greater self-awareness and a deeper understanding of one's strengths, weaknesses, and areas for improvement.

Improved relationships: People with a growth mindset are more likely to engage in constructive communication and seek out opportunities for collaboration and growth in their relationships. This can lead to stronger and more fulfilling personal and professional relationships.

A growth mindset is a way of thinking and approaching life that is focused on growth, learning, and development. People with a growth mindset believe that their abilities and talents can be developed through hard work, effort, and perseverance, and they are more likely to embrace challenges, view failure as a learning opportunity, value effort and perseverance

Differences between a growth and fixed mindset

The concepts of growth mindset and fixed mindset were first introduced by psychologist Carol Dweck in her book, "Mindset: The New Psychology of Success." These mindsets describe two different approaches to life, which can have a significant impact on how individuals approach challenges, setbacks, and opportunities for growth and development.

A growth mindset is characterized by the belief that abilities and talents can be developed and improved through effort, hard work, and perseverance. People with a growth mindset tend to see challenges as opportunities for growth and learning, and they are more likely to embrace failure as a natural part of the learning process. In contrast, a fixed mindset is characterized by the belief that abilities and talents are fixed and unchanging. People with a fixed mindset tend to see challenges as threats to their sense of self-worth and are more likely to avoid failure at all costs.

There are several key differences between a growth and fixed mindset, which can have significant implications for personal and professional success. Some of the key differences include:

Approach to Challenges: People with a growth mindset tend to approach challenges as opportunities for growth and learning, while those with a fixed mindset may view challenges as threats to their sense of self-worth. People with a growth mindset are more likely to embrace challenges and persist in the face of setbacks, while those with a fixed mindset may be more likely to avoid challenges and give up when faced with difficulty.

Perception of Failure: People with a growth mindset tend to view failure as a natural part of the learning process, while those with a fixed mindset may see failure as a reflection of their abilities or worth as a person. People with a growth mindset are more likely to learn from their mistakes and use these experiences to improve their performance in the future, while those with a fixed mindset may be more likely to give up after experiencing failure.

Belief in Effort and Perseverance: People with a growth mindset believe that hard work, effort, and perseverance are essential for achieving success, while those with a fixed mindset may believe that success is predetermined and cannot be influenced by effort. People with a growth mindset are more likely to put in the necessary time and effort to achieve their goals, while those with a fixed mindset may be more likely to give up if success is not immediate.

Response to Feedback: People with a growth mindset are open to feedback and seek out opportunities for learning and development, while those with a fixed mindset may be more resistant to feedback that challenges their beliefs about their abilities. People with a growth mindset are more likely to seek feedback from others, ask questions, and engage in self-reflection to identify areas for improvement, while those with a fixed mindset may be more likely to dismiss feedback that does not align with their beliefs.

Belief in Learning and Growth: People with a growth mindset believe that they can learn and grow over time, while those with a fixed mindset may believe that their abilities and talents are predetermined and cannot be changed. People with a growth mindset are more likely to seek out opportunities for learning and development, while those with a fixed mindset may be more likely to avoid new experiences or challenges that may challenge their sense of self-worth.

The implications of these differences can be significant for personal and professional success. People with a growth mindset are more likely to achieve success in a variety of areas, including academics, athletics, and personal relationships. By focusing on learning and improvement, rather than avoiding failure, they are more likely to take on challenges and persist in the face of setbacks, leading to improved performance over time.

In contrast, people with a fixed mindset may be more prone to giving up when faced with challenges or setbacks, which can limit their potential for growth and development. They may also be more likely to avoid new experiences or challenges that may challenge their sense of

Techniques to develop a growth mindset

Self-worth, limiting their opportunities for learning and personal growth

Additionally, people with a fixed mindset may struggle with receiving feedback or constructive criticism, as they may see it as a threat to their self-concept. This can make it difficult for them to identify areas for improvement or seek out opportunities for learning and development, which can ultimately limit their potential for success.

On the other hand, people with a growth mindset are more likely to embrace feedback and use it as an opportunity for learning and growth. They are also more likely to seek out new experiences and challenges, as they see these opportunities as a chance to develop and improve their skills and abilities.

It's important to note that people can have different mindsets in different areas of their lives. For example, someone may have a growth mindset when it comes to academics but a fixed mindset when it comes to personal relationships. Recognizing these differences and working to cultivate a growth mindset in all areas of life can be a powerful tool for personal and professional success.

To cultivate a growth mindset, it's important to focus on the following strategies:

Embrace challenges: Instead of avoiding challenges, see them as opportunities for growth and development. This means pushing yourself out of your comfort zone and taking on new experiences, even if they feel intimidating or unfamiliar.

Emphasize effort: Rather than focusing on natural talents or abilities, emphasize the importance of effort and hard work in achieving success. Recognize that success is a result of persistence and dedication, rather than innate talent.

Learn from failure: Embrace failure as a natural part of the learning process, and use these experiences to identify areas for improvement and growth. Recognize that failure is not a reflection of your worth as a person, but rather an opportunity to learn and grow.

Seek out feedback: Be open to receiving feedback and constructive criticism, and use it as an opportunity to learn and grow. Recognize that feedback is not a threat to your self-concept, but rather a chance to improve your skills and abilities.

Cultivate a love of learning: Emphasize the importance of learning and personal growth, and seek out opportunities for continuous learning and development. This may involve taking courses, attending workshops, or simply exploring new interests and hobbies.

By focusing on these strategies, it's possible to cultivate a growth mindset and reap the many benefits that come with it. From improved performance and increased resilience to greater personal fulfillment and satisfaction, a growth mindset can be a powerful tool for personal and professional success.

Chapter 5

EMBRACING CHANGE

C hange is an inevitable part of life, and yet it can often be difficult and unsettling. Whether it's a major life change such as a job loss or a relationship ending, or a more minor change such as moving to a new city or starting a new hobby, change can be stressful and overwhelming.

There are a number of reasons why change can be difficult, including:

Fear of the unknown: When we are faced with change, we are often confronted with the unknown. We don't know what the future will hold or how we will adapt to the new situation. This uncertainty can be scary and make us feel anxious or stressed.

Loss of control: Change can often feel like it is happening to us, rather than being within our control. This can leave us feeling powerless and overwhelmed.

Discomfort with change: For some people, change simply feels uncomfortable. They may be resistant to new experiences or routines and feel more comfortable with the familiar.

Loss and grief: Even positive changes can involve a sense of loss or grief. For example, a promotion at work may involve leaving behind familiar coworkers and routines, or moving to a new city may mean leaving behind friends and family.

Attachment to the past: We may feel attached to our past experiences or way of life, and find it difficult to let go of them. This attachment can make it hard to embrace new experiences and opportunities.

Despite these challenges, change can also bring about a number of positive outcomes, including personal growth, new opportunities, and increased resilience. Learning to embrace change and adapt to new situations can be an important tool for personal and professional success.

Strategies to embrace change

Change is a natural part of life, but it can often be difficult to embrace. Whether it's a change in career, a move to a new city, or a shift in personal relationships, change can be challenging to navigate. However, there are strategies that can help you to embrace change and approach it with a positive and optimistic mindset.

Accept and Acknowledge Your Feelings

One of the first steps to embracing change is to acknowledge and accept the feelings that come with it. Change can be unsettling and even stressful, and it's normal to feel a range of emotions like fear, anxiety, or sadness. It's important to recognize that these feelings are natural and to give yourself space to process them.

Practice Self-Compassion

Self-compassion involves being kind and understanding towards yourself, particularly during difficult times. By practicing self-compassion, you can give yourself the support and understanding needed to navigate change. This can involve things like reminding yourself that it's okay to make mistakes or being patient with yourself as you adjust to new circumstances.

Focus on the Positives

While change can be unsettling, it can also bring about positive outcomes and opportunities. By focusing on the positive aspects of the change, you can help yourself to approach it with a more optimistic mindset. This can involve making a list of potential benefits, such as new experiences, skills, or relationships.

Set Realistic Expectations

It's important to set realistic expectations for yourself as you navigate change. Change can be difficult, and it's unlikely that everything will go smoothly right away. By setting realistic expectations, you can reduce the pressure you put on yourself and approach the change with greater flexibility and patience.

Seek Support

Navigating change can be challenging, and it's important to seek support from others. This could involve talking to friends or family, joining a support group, or seeing a therapist. By reaching out to others, you can gain perspective on the change and receive emotional support and guidance.

Build Resilience

Resilience refers to the ability to bounce back from difficult experiences. By building resilience, you can approach change with greater flexibility and adaptability. Strategies for building resilience include cultivating a growth mindset, engaging in self-care practices, and practicing mindfulness.

Take Small Steps

Embracing change doesn't mean jumping in headfirst. It's okay to take small steps towards the change, whether that means exploring new job opportunities or gradually adjusting to a new living situation. By taking small steps, you can reduce the stress and anxiety associated with change and build confidence in your ability to adapt.

Learn from Past Experiences

If you've navigated change in the past, reflect on what worked well and what didn't. This can help you to approach the current change with a greater sense of confidence and understanding. By learning from past experiences, you can build resilience and approach change with greater ease.

Stay Positive

Finally, it's important to maintain a positive mindset as you navigate change. This can involve reframing negative thoughts or self-talk, focusing on the positives, and practicing gratitude. By staying positive, you can approach change with greater ease and optimism.

Embracing change can be challenging, but it's an important part of personal growth and development. By practicing self-compassion, seeking support, and staying positive, you can approach change with greater ease and adaptability. Remember, change can bring about positive outcomes and opportunities, and by embracing it, you can learn and grow in ways you may never have imagined.

The importance of being adaptable and flexible

Being adaptable and flexible is an important characteristic for personal growth and success in many aspects of life. Whether it's in the workplace, personal relationships, or personal development, being able to adapt to changing circumstances is crucial. In this article, we'll explore the importance of being adaptable and flexible and provide strategies for cultivating these traits.

Adaptability and Flexibility Defined

Adaptability is the ability to adjust to new or changing situations, while flexibility is the ability to change or modify one's thinking, behavior, or approach to a situation. Both traits are closely related and involve being able to handle uncertainty, ambiguity, and change.

Benefits of Being Adaptable and Flexible

Being adaptable and flexible can bring about a range of benefits, including:

Improved problem-solving skills: Being adaptable and flexible can help you to approach problems with creativity and innovation, allowing you to find unique solutions to complex issues.

Increased resilience: Adaptable and flexible people are better equipped to bounce back from setbacks and challenges, as they can adjust their thinking and behavior to new circumstances.

Greater career success: In the workplace, adaptable and flexible employees are highly valued for their ability to handle change and uncertainty, making them more likely to succeed and advance in their careers.

Stronger personal relationships: Adaptable and flexible people are better equipped to navigate interpersonal relationships, as they can adjust their behavior and approach to accommodate others' needs and preferences.

Improved overall wellbeing: Being adaptable and flexible can lead to greater resilience, reduced stress, and improved mental and physical health.

Strategies for Cultivating Adaptability and Flexibility

If you want to develop your adaptability and flexibility, here are some strategies to consider:

Embrace change: One of the most effective ways to cultivate adaptability and flexibility is to embrace change. This can involve intentionally seeking out new experiences, exploring different perspectives, and being open to new ideas and approaches.

Develop a growth mindset: A growth mindset involves believing that your abilities and skills can be developed through effort and perseverance. By cultivating a growth mindset, you can approach new challenges with a sense of curiosity and openness, rather than fear and uncertainty.

Practice mindfulness: Mindfulness involves being present in the moment and non-judgmentally observing your thoughts and feelings. By practicing mindfulness, you can increase your awareness of your own reactions to change and develop greater self-control over your responses.

Build resilience: Resilience involves being able to bounce back from setbacks and challenges. By cultivating resilience, you can approach change with greater ease and adaptability. Strategies for building resilience include practicing self-care, maintaining social connections, and reframing negative thinking.

Learn from past experiences: If you've navigated change in the past, reflect on what worked well and what didn't. This can help you to approach future changes with a greater sense of confidence and understanding.

Stay curious: Being curious involves being interested in learning new things and exploring new perspectives. By staying curious, you can approach change with a sense of excitement and adventure, rather than fear and uncertainty.

Challenges to Being Adaptable and Flexible

While being adaptable and flexible is important, it's not always easy. There are several challenges that can make it difficult to cultivate these traits, including:

Fear of the unknown: Many people are uncomfortable with uncertainty and the unknown. This can make it difficult to embrace change and be adaptable and flexible.

Rigidity in thinking: Some people may have a rigid way of thinking or fixed ideas about how things should be done. This can make it challenging to be adaptable and flexible, as they may struggle to adjust their thinking or behavior to new circumstances.

Lack of self-awareness: If you're not aware of your own thinking patterns or behaviors, it can be difficult to recognize.

Adaptability and flexibility are important qualities to possess in both personal and professional contexts. In an ever-changing world, those who can adapt quickly and easily to new circumstances and challenges are more likely to succeed and thrive. Here are some additional points to consider:

Adaptable people are open to new experiences and ideas. They are willing to try new things and take calculated risks. They are not afraid of failure because they see it as an opportunity to learn and grow.

Adaptable people are resilient. They bounce back quickly from setbacks and are able to maintain a positive attitude even in difficult situations.

Adaptable people are good problem-solvers. They are able to think creatively and come up with innovative solutions to challenges.

Adaptable people are good at building relationships. They are able to communicate effectively with others and build strong networks of support.

Adaptable people are able to balance competing priorities. They are able to prioritize their time and resources effectively and make decisions quickly and confidently.

Adaptable people are able to stay calm under pressure. They are able to manage their emotions and maintain their composure even in stressful situations.

Adaptable people are able to learn quickly. They are able to absorb new information and skills quickly and apply them effectively.

Adaptable people are able to stay focused on their goals. They are able to adapt their strategies and tactics as needed to achieve their goals.

Overall, being adaptable and flexible is critical to success in both personal and professional contexts. By developing these qualities, you can become more resilient, better at problem-solving, and more effective at achieving your goals.

Chapter 6

SETTING GOALS

Setting goals is a crucial aspect of personal and professional development. Goals provide direction, motivation, and a sense of purpose. They help individuals clarify what they want to achieve, identify the steps needed to get there, and measure their progress along the way. Here are some reasons why setting goals is important:

Goals provide direction and focus: Without goals, individuals can feel aimless, unsure of where they are headed, and may struggle to make decisions. Setting goals provides clarity and direction, helping individuals to focus their energy and resources on what is most important.

Goals motivate and inspire: Having a clear goal to work towards can be incredibly motivating. Goals provide a sense of purpose, inspire individuals to work harder and smarter, and can help them overcome obstacles and setbacks along the way.

Goals provide a sense of accomplishment: When individuals achieve their goals, it can be incredibly satisfying and rewarding. Setting and achieving goals helps individuals build self-confidence, a sense of competence, and a belief in their own abilities.

Goals help individuals prioritize: With so many demands on our time and attention, it can be challenging to determine what is most important. Setting goals helps individuals prioritize their time, resources, and efforts to achieve what is most important to them.

Goals provide a roadmap: Setting goals provides a roadmap for achieving what we want. Goals help individuals identify the steps needed to get there, track progress, and make adjustments along the way.

Goals provide a measure of progress: Setting goals helps individuals measure progress towards what they want to achieve. By tracking progress, individuals can see how far they have come, celebrate their successes, and identify areas where they need to improve.

Goals help individuals stretch and grow: Setting goals that are challenging but achievable can help individuals stretch and grow beyond their current limits. Working towards goals requires individuals to learn new skills, take risks, and push themselves outside their comfort zone.

Goals provide a sense of accountability: Setting goals provides a sense of accountability to oneself and others. By setting goals and sharing them with others, individuals are more likely to follow through on their commitments and achieve what they set out to do.

Overall, setting goals is an important aspect of personal and professional development. Goals provide direction, motivation, a sense of accomplishment, and a roadmap for achieving what we want. By setting goals, individuals can prioritize, measure progress, stretch and grow, and build a sense of accountability.

How to set effective goals?

Setting effective goals is crucial for achieving success, both personally and professionally. Here are some guidelines on how to set effective goals:

Be specific: Goals should be specific and well-defined. Vague goals such as "lose weight" or "improve my career" are difficult to achieve because they lack clarity. Instead, set specific goals such as "lose 10 pounds in three months" or "earn a promotion within the next year."

Make goals measurable: Goals should be measurable so that you can track your progress and evaluate your success. This means setting clear metrics for success, such as hitting a certain revenue target, completing a certain number of projects, or running a certain distance.

Make goals challenging but achievable: Goals should be challenging enough to push you outside of your comfort zone but still achievable. Setting goals that are too easy won't provide much motivation, while setting goals that are impossible to achieve will lead to frustration and discouragement.

Set realistic timelines: Goals should have realistic timelines that take into account your resources and available time. Setting an unrealistic timeline will likely result in failure and frustration.

Write down your goals: Writing down your goals helps to solidify them in your mind and increases your commitment to achieving them. Put your goals somewhere visible, such as on your desk or refrigerator, as a reminder to stay focused.

Break down larger goals into smaller ones: Larger goals can feel overwhelming, so it's important to break them down into smaller, manageable steps. This also allows you to track progress and celebrate smaller successes along the way.

Share your goals with others: Sharing your goals with friends, family, or a mentor can provide a sense of accountability and support. They can also offer feedback and guidance to help you achieve your goals.

Evaluate and adjust goals as needed: As you work towards your goals, it's important to evaluate your progress and adjust your goals as necessary. This may involve changing your timeline, revising your metrics, or adjusting your approach.

Stay flexible: Unexpected challenges and opportunities can arise, so it's important to stay flexible and adjust your goals as needed. This may involve changing the specific goal or adjusting your timeline.

By following these guidelines, you can set effective goals that will help you achieve success and personal growth. Remember to stay focused, stay committed, and stay flexible as you work towards your goals.

Benefits of achieving goals

Achieving goals is an essential aspect of personal and professional growth. Setting goals provides direction, motivation, and focus, and achieving them can bring a sense of accomplishment, fulfillment, and satisfaction. Here are some benefits of achieving goals:

Increases self-confidence: Accomplishing a goal can boost self-confidence and self-esteem, as it validates your ability to succeed and overcome obstacles. This can lead to an increased sense of self-worth and a positive outlook on future endeavors.

Provides motivation: Setting and achieving goals can provide motivation to continue striving towards success. It creates a sense of purpose and direction, which can help to overcome procrastination and other barriers to productivity.

Enhances decision-making skills: Pursuing a goal requires making decisions that will move you closer to achieving it. This can enhance decision-making skills by forcing you to weigh the pros and cons of different options and make informed choices.

Improves focus: Goals provide clarity and focus, allowing you to direct your energy and resources towards a specific objective. This can increase productivity and efficiency by eliminating distractions and improving time management.

Develops resilience: Pursuing a goal often involves overcoming obstacles and setbacks. This can develop resilience and perseverance, allowing you to bounce back from challenges and continue moving forward.

Fosters personal growth: Achieving goals often involves acquiring new skills and knowledge, which can lead to personal growth and development. This can increase your confidence, broaden your perspectives, and enhance your sense of purpose and meaning in life.

Builds credibility: Accomplishing goals can build credibility and reputation, both personally and professionally. It demonstrates your ability to follow through on commitments and achieve results, which can enhance your standing in your community, industry, or field.

Provides a sense of accomplishment: Accomplishing a goal can provide a sense of accomplishment and fulfillment, which can improve overall well-being and life satisfaction. It can also be a source of inspiration for future endeavors, as it shows that with effort and dedication, you can achieve your objectives.

Creates positive habits: Pursuing a goal often involves developing positive habits, such as discipline, perseverance, and consistency. These habits can translate into other areas of your life, leading to further personal and professional growth.

Achieving goals is an essential part of personal and professional growth. It provides motivation, focus, and direction, and can enhance self-confidence, decision-making skills, resilience, and personal growth. Whether big or small, accomplishing goals can bring a sense of accomplishment and fulfillment, and set the stage for continued success in the future.

Chapter 7

DEVELOPING RESILIENCE

Resilience is the ability to adapt and bounce back from difficult situations, setbacks, and adversity. It is the capacity to maintain mental and emotional strength and stability, even in the face of challenges and stressors. Resilience is not a fixed trait or characteristic; rather, it is a dynamic process that can be developed and strengthened through intentional effort and practice.

Resilience involves several key components:

Adaptability: Resilient individuals are adaptable and flexible, able to adjust to changing circumstances and find creative solutions to problems. They are not rigid in their thinking or behaviors, but rather open to new ideas and ways of doing things.

Coping skills: Resilient individuals have effective coping skills, including positive self-talk, stress reduction techniques, and problem-solving strategies. They are able to manage their emotions and reactions in a healthy and constructive way, rather than becoming overwhelmed or reactive.

Support systems: Resilient individuals have a strong network of support, including family, friends, colleagues, and professionals.

They are able to lean on others for emotional and practical support when needed, and also provide support to others in return.

Self-efficacy: Resilient individuals have a strong sense of self-efficacy, or belief in their ability to handle challenges and achieve their goals. They have a growth mindset, viewing challenges as opportunities for growth and learning rather than insurmountable obstacles.

There are several factors that can contribute to resilience, including:

Positive relationships: Having positive and supportive relationships with family, friends, and colleagues can provide a sense of connection and belonging, as well as practical and emotional support during difficult times.

Sense of purpose: Having a sense of purpose and meaning in life can provide motivation and direction, and help individuals stay focused on their goals even in the face of adversity.

Positive self-image: Having a positive self-image and high self-esteem can increase resilience, as individuals are better able to cope with stress and challenges when they feel confident and capable.

Effective coping skills: Developing effective coping skills, such as mindfulness, relaxation techniques, and problem-solving strategies, can help individuals manage stress and anxiety and build resilience.

Healthy lifestyle habits: Maintaining a healthy lifestyle, including regular exercise, healthy eating habits, and adequate sleep, can support physical and mental health and increase resilience.

Resilience is a critical component of mental and emotional well-being, enabling individuals to adapt and bounce back from difficult situations and challenges. It involves several key components, including adaptability, coping skills, support systems, and self-efficacy. While some individuals may have a natural propensity for resilience, it is a dynamic process that can be developed and strengthened through intentional effort and practice, as well as through positive relationships, a sense of purpose, a positive self-image, effective coping skills, and healthy lifestyle habits.

The importance of resilience

Resilience is a critical component of mental and emotional well-being, enabling individuals to adapt and bounce back from difficult situations and challenges. It is particularly important in today's rapidly changing and unpredictable world, where individuals are faced with a wide range of stressors and uncertainties.

There are several key reasons why resilience is important:

Coping with adversity: Resilience enables individuals to cope with adversity and stress, whether it be a major life change, a challenging work situation, or a personal crisis. Individuals who are resilient are better equipped to handle stressors and bounce back from setbacks, rather than becoming overwhelmed or discouraged.

Improving mental health: Resilience can also improve mental health outcomes, reducing the risk of developing anxiety, depression, and other mental health conditions. It can provide a sense of control and mastery over one's circumstances, increasing feelings of self-efficacy and confidence.

Enhancing physical health: Resilience is also linked to physical health outcomes, as individuals who are resilient are better able to cope with chronic illness and physical stressors. They are more likely to engage in healthy behaviors, such as regular exercise and healthy eating habits, which can reduce the risk of chronic diseases.

Boosting performance: Resilience can also enhance performance, whether it be in the workplace or in personal endeavors. Individuals who are resilient are better able to handle pressure and uncertainty, and are more likely to persist in the face of challenges and setbacks.

Building relationships: Resilience can also improve relationships, as individuals who are resilient are better able to communicate effectively, handle conflict, and provide emotional support to others. They are more likely to form positive relationships and maintain them over time.

There are several strategies that individuals can use to build resilience, including:

Developing positive self-talk: Individuals can build resilience by developing positive self-talk, or inner dialogue that is supportive and encouraging. This can involve reframing negative thoughts and focusing on strengths and past successes.

Building a support system: Building a strong network of support, including family, friends, and colleagues, can provide emotional and practical support during difficult times. Support groups and professional counseling can also be helpful.

Practicing mindfulness: Mindfulness practices, such as meditation and deep breathing, can help individuals manage stress and anxiety, and build resilience over time.

Pursuing meaningful activities: Engaging in meaningful activities and hobbies can provide a sense of purpose and fulfillment, and help individuals stay focused on their goals.

Maintaining a healthy lifestyle: Maintaining a healthy lifestyle, including regular exercise, healthy eating habits, and adequate sleep, can support physical and mental health, and increase resilience over time.

Resilience is a critical component of mental and emotional well-being, enabling individuals to adapt and bounce back from difficult situations and challenges. It is particularly important in today's rapidly changing and unpredictable world, and can improve mental and physical health outcomes, enhance performance, build relationships, and provide a sense of control and mastery over one's circumstances. By developing strategies to build resilience, individuals can better cope with stressors and challenges, and live happier and more fulfilling lives.

Techniques to develop resilience

Resilience is the ability to recover and adapt to difficult situations. Developing resilience can be an important tool in managing stress and overcoming adversity. While some people may naturally be more resilient than others, resilience can also be learned and practiced. Here are some techniques that can help develop resilience:

Practice Mindfulness

Mindfulness involves being present in the moment, observing and accepting one's thoughts and emotions without judgment. It can help build resilience by allowing individuals to recognize and manage their stressors in a healthy way. Mindfulness can be practiced through meditation, yoga, or simply taking a few deep breaths and focusing on the present moment.

Develop a Positive Mindset

Resilient individuals often have a positive outlook and are able to reframe negative experiences as opportunities for growth. Developing a positive mindset can be done through positive self-talk, gratitude journaling, and focusing on personal strengths and achievements.

Build Strong Relationships

Having a support network of friends, family, and colleagues can be crucial in developing resilience. Strong relationships can provide emotional support, guidance, and practical assistance during difficult times. Investing time and effort into building and maintaining relationships can be a powerful tool in developing resilience.

Practice Self-Care

Self-care is any activity that promotes physical, emotional, or mental well-being. It can include things like exercise, healthy eating, getting enough sleep, and taking time for hobbies or relaxation. Practicing self-care can help individuals manage stress and build resilience by allowing them to prioritize their own well-being.

Set Realistic Goals

Having clear goals and a plan for achieving them can help individuals feel more in control of their lives and build resilience. However, it's important to set realistic goals that are achievable within a reasonable timeframe. Setting goals that are too lofty or unrealistic can lead to frustration and feelings of failure, which can undermine resilience.

Learn from Failure

Resilient individuals are able to learn from their failures and use them as opportunities for growth. Instead of dwelling on mistakes or setbacks, try to identify what went wrong and how you can do better in the future. This can help build resilience and confidence in your ability to overcome challenges.

Flexibility

Flexibility involves being able to adapt to changing situations and adjust your expectations accordingly. This can be particularly important in developing resilience, as unexpected events can often derail progress towards goals. Practicing flexibility can involve being open to new ideas and perspectives, as well as being willing to change course when necessary.

Seek Professional

Help Sometimes, building resilience may require the help of a professional. This can include seeking therapy or counseling to work through difficult emotions and experiences, or consulting with a career coach or mentor to develop new skills and strategies for achieving goals. Seeking professional help is a sign of strength and can be an important step in developing resilience.

Developing resilience can be an important tool in managing stress and overcoming adversity. While some people may naturally be more resilient than others, resilience can also be learned and practiced through techniques like mindfulness, positive thinking, building strong relationships, self-care, setting realistic goals, and learning from failure, practicing flexibility, and seeking professional help. By incorporating these strategies into their daily lives, individuals can develop the skills and mindset necessary to bounce back from difficult experiences and achieve their goals.

Chapter 8

BUILDING CONFIDENCE

Confidence can be defined as a belief in one's abilities, qualities, and judgment. It is an essential trait that can help individuals achieve their goals, take risks, and overcome obstacles. Having confidence can improve one's mental and emotional well-being, relationships, and overall quality of life.

Confidence is important because it can influence how an individual sees themselves and how others perceive them. When individuals are confident, they exude a sense of self-assurance, which can help them command respect and be taken seriously. It can also help individuals feel empowered to take on new challenges and pursue their goals.

Additionally, confidence can improve an individual's ability to cope with stress and setbacks. When individuals are confident, they are more likely to view obstacles as temporary setbacks rather than insurmountable barriers. This mindset can help individuals stay motivated and focused on their goals, even in the face of adversity.

In the workplace, confidence is often seen as a desirable trait, particularly in leadership positions. A confident leader can inspire and motivate their team, leading to improved performance and productivity. Additionally, confident employees are more likely to take on new projects and initiatives, leading to growth and development for themselves and the organization.

In relationships, confidence can help individuals communicate their needs and desires effectively, leading to healthier and more fulfilling connections. Individuals who are confident in themselves are less likely to seek validation from others, leading to more authentic and satisfying relationships.

Overall, confidence is an essential trait that can improve an individual's mental and emotional well-being, relationships, and overall quality of life. It can help individuals achieve their goals, take on new challenges, and overcome obstacles with resilience and determination.

In the next section, we will explore some strategies for building confidence.

Strategies to build self-confidence

Building self-confidence can be challenging, particularly for individuals who struggle with self-doubt or have experienced setbacks or failures. However, there are several strategies that individuals can use to build their confidence and improve their sense of self-worth.

Identify and challenge negative self-talk: Negative self-talk can be a significant barrier to building confidence. When individuals engage in negative self-talk, they reinforce negative beliefs about themselves, which can erode their sense of self-worth. To combat negative self-talk, individuals can start by identifying negative self-talk patterns and challenging them with positive self-talk. For example, if an individual thinks, "I'll never be able to do this," they can challenge that thought with "I may struggle at first, but with practice and perseverance, I can learn and grow."

Set achievable goals: Setting achievable goals can help individuals build confidence by providing a sense of accomplishment and progress. When individuals achieve their goals, they reinforce a sense of competence and capability, which can improve their self-confidence. However, it's important to set goals that are realistic and achievable to avoid setting oneself up for failure.

Practice self-care: Self-care is an essential aspect of building confidence. When individuals take care of themselves physically, emotionally, and mentally, they reinforce a sense of self-worth and self-respect. This can involve practicing healthy habits, such as getting enough sleep, exercising regularly, and eating a balanced diet. It can also involve engaging in activities that bring joy and fulfillment, such as hobbies, socializing, or spending time in nature.

Celebrate successes: Celebrating successes, no matter how small, can help individuals build confidence and reinforce positive self-beliefs. When individuals acknowledge their accomplishments, they reinforce a sense of competence and achievement, which can improve their self-confidence. Celebrating successes can involve rewarding oneself for a job well done, sharing accomplishments with friends or loved ones, or simply taking a moment to reflect on what was achieved.

Practice self-compassion: Self-compassion is a crucial aspect of building confidence. When individuals practice self-compassion, they learn to treat themselves with kindness, understanding, and forgiveness. This can involve acknowledging one's mistakes and shortcomings without judgment and offering oneself empathy and support. Practicing self-compassion can help individuals build a sense of self-worth and reduce self-doubt and negative self-talk.

Step out of one's comfort zone: Stepping out of one's comfort zone can be a powerful way to build confidence. When individuals challenge themselves to try new things or take on new challenges, they reinforce a sense of competence and capability. Stepping out of one's comfort zone can involve trying new activities, taking on new responsibilities at work, or facing fears or phobias.

Surround one with positive influences: Surrounding oneself with positive influences can help build confidence by providing a supportive and encouraging environment. This can involve spending time with friends and loved ones who offer positive feedback and encouragement or seeking out mentors or role models who inspire and motivate.

Practice visualization: Visualization is a powerful tool that can help individuals build confidence by imagining themselves succeeding in a particular area. Visualization involves creating a mental image of oneself achieving a goal or performing well in a challenging situation. This can help individuals build confidence by reinforcing positive self-beliefs and reducing anxiety and self-doubt.

Building self-confidence is an essential aspect of personal growth and development. It can improve an individual's mental and emotional well-being, relationships, and overall quality of life. By identifying and challenging negative self-talk, setting achievable goals, practicing self-care, celebrating successes, practicing self-compassion, stepping out of one's comfort zone, surrounding oneself with positive influences, and practicing visualization, individuals can build their confidence and

The benefits of being confident

Confidence is an essential trait that can significantly influence various aspects of an individual's life, including personal relationships, career, and mental health. Confident people have higher self-esteem, are more assertive, and are better able to navigate challenges and obstacles. In this article, we will explore the benefits of being confident and how it can positively impact an individual's life.

Better mental health: Confidence is linked to better mental health, as it helps individuals feel better about themselves and their abilities. People with confidence are more likely to have a positive outlook on life, be optimistic, and have higher self-esteem. This can help them deal with stress, anxiety, and depression more effectively.

Improved relationships: Confident individuals are better equipped to navigate relationships and social situations. They are more likely to be assertive, communicate their needs and boundaries effectively, and build stronger, healthier relationships. People who lack confidence may struggle with social anxiety or avoid social situations altogether, making it challenging to form and maintain relationships.

Enhanced career success: Confidence is a crucial trait for success in the workplace. Confident individuals are more likely to take on new challenges, ask for raises or promotions, and advocate for themselves in the workplace. They are also more likely to be viewed as competent and capable by their colleagues, which can lead to more significant career opportunities.

Increased creativity: Confident individuals are more likely to take risks, explore new ideas, and think outside of the box. They are less likely to be held back by fear or self-doubt, allowing them to tap into their creativity and innovation.

Improved decision-making: Confident individuals are more decisive and better equipped to make tough decisions. They trust their instincts and are less likely to second-guess themselves, which can help them make more informed and effective decisions.

Better physical health: Confident individuals are more likely to take care of their physical health. They are more likely to exercise regularly, eat a healthy diet, and prioritize their overall well-being.

Increased happiness: Confidence is linked to greater happiness and life satisfaction. People who are confident in themselves and their abilities are more likely to feel fulfilled and satisfied with their lives.

Overall, confidence is an essential trait that can have a significant impact on an individual's life. It can improve mental and physical health, enhance career success, improve relationships, increase creativity, and lead to greater happiness and life satisfaction. If you struggle with confidence, there are various strategies and techniques you can use to build your self-esteem and cultivate greater confidence in yourself and your abilities.

Chapter 9

ENHANCING EMOTIONAL INTELLIGENCE

E motional intelligence (EI) refers to the ability to perceive, understand, manage, and express one's emotions effectively, as well as to perceive, understand, and influence the emotions of others. It involves using emotional information to guide thinking and behavior, and it encompasses a range of skills and abilities that relate to emotional awareness, emotional regulation, empathy, and social skills.

Emotional intelligence has become increasingly recognized as an important factor in personal and professional success, and research has shown that individuals with high levels of EI tend to have better mental health, stronger relationships, and more effective leadership skills than those with lower levels of EI.

The concept of emotional intelligence was first introduced by psychologists Peter Salovey and John Mayer in 1990, and it gained widespread attention after the publication of Daniel Goleman's book "Emotional Intelligence" in 1995.

There are a few different models of emotional intelligence, but one of the most widely recognized is the one developed by Goleman, which includes five components:

Self-awareness: The ability to recognize and understand one's own emotions and their effects on oneself and others.

Self-regulation: The ability to manage one's own emotions, thoughts, and behaviors in a constructive manner.

Motivation: The ability to channel emotions towards achieving goals and pursuing interests.

Empathy: The ability to understand and relate to the emotions and perspectives of others.

Social skills: The ability to build and maintain positive relationships and communicate effectively with others.

Together, these components make up a comprehensive framework for understanding emotional intelligence and its impact on various aspects of life.

Developing emotional intelligence requires a combination of self-reflection, self-awareness, and practice. By becoming more aware of one's own emotions and learning to regulate them in a constructive manner, individuals can improve their ability to manage stress, handle conflicts, and build strong relationships.

In addition, developing empathy and social skills can help individuals to understand and connect with others more effectively, which can lead to better communication, collaboration, and teamwork. Overall, emotional intelligence is an important factor in personal and professional success, and investing in its development can have significant benefits for individuals and those around them.

Why emotional intelligence is important

Emotional intelligence is an important trait that has been shown to have a significant impact on both personal and professional success. Here are some reasons why emotional intelligence is important:

Better Mental Health: Emotional intelligence can help individuals manage their emotions and reduce stress, leading to better mental health. Research has shown that individuals with high levels of emotional intelligence tend to experience less anxiety, depression, and other negative emotions.

Improved Relationships: Emotional intelligence can help individuals build strong and positive relationships with others. By understanding and empathizing with others' emotions, individuals can communicate more effectively, resolve conflicts more easily, and build deeper connections with those around them.

Enhanced Leadership Skills: Emotional intelligence is an important factor in effective leadership. Leaders who are able to understand and manage their own emotions, as well as those of their team members, are better able to inspire and motivate others, build strong relationships, and make sound decisions.

Increased Job Performance: Emotional intelligence has been linked to better job performance across a variety of fields. Individuals with high levels of emotional intelligence tend to be more adaptable, creative, and productive, and are better able to work in teams and communicate effectively with others.

Higher Emotional Resilience: Emotional intelligence can help individuals cope with stress and adversity, leading to greater emotional resilience. By understanding and regulating their own emotions, individuals can better manage stress and bounce back from setbacks and challenges.

Better Conflict Resolution: Emotional intelligence can help individuals resolve conflicts more effectively. By understanding and empathizing with the emotions of others, individuals can communicate more effectively, find common ground, and work towards a resolution that benefits everyone involved.

Overall, emotional intelligence is an important trait that can have a significant impact on various aspects of life. Developing emotional intelligence requires self-awareness, empathy, and practice, but the benefits are well worth the effort. By becoming more emotionally intelligent, individuals can lead happier, healthier, and more successful lives.

Techniques to enhance emotional intelligence

Enhancing emotional intelligence can be a valuable tool in personal and professional growth. Here are some techniques to help develop and enhance emotional intelligence:

Practice Self-Awareness: Self-awareness is the foundation of emotional intelligence. It involves being in tune with your own emotions and understanding how they impact your thoughts and behavior. Practice self-reflection and self-examination to identify your emotions and triggers.

Cultivate Empathy: Empathy is the ability to understand and share the feelings of others. Practice putting yourself in other people's shoes and trying to understand their perspectives. This can help you better understand and communicate with others.

Improve Active Listening Skills: Active listening involves fully focusing on what someone is saying, both verbally and non-verbally. It involves listening without judgment, interrupting or getting defensive. This can help build deeper connections with others and better understand their emotions.

Develop Emotional Regulation Skills: Emotional regulation involves managing your emotions in a healthy and productive way. This can include deep breathing exercises, mindfulness practices, and stress reduction techniques such as meditation.

Practice Positive Self-Talk: The way we talk to ourselves can impact our emotions and behavior. Practice positive self-talk to build self-confidence and a positive mindset. This can help you better manage stress and build emotional resilience.

Develop Interpersonal Communication Skills: Effective communication involves not only verbal but also non-verbal cues such as facial expressions, tone of voice and body language. Practice communication techniques such as active listening, asking open-ended questions, and being assertive when necessary.

Develop Social Skills: Social skills involve building strong relationships and connecting with others. This can include networking, building rapport, and developing a sense of humor to diffuse tense situations.

Seek Feedback and Be Open to Criticism: Feedback from others can help you better understand your own emotions and how they impact others. Be open to constructive criticism and seek feedback from others to develop a better sense of self-awareness and improve interpersonal skills.

Practice Mindfulness: Mindfulness is a practice that involves being present in the moment and fully experiencing your surroundings. It can help improve emotional regulation and reduce stress.

Learn to Manage Conflict: Conflict can arise in any situation, and emotional intelligence can help you navigate difficult conversations and resolve conflict in a healthy way. Practice active listening, staying calm and assertive, and seeking common ground to resolve conflicts effectively.

Developing emotional intelligence takes time and effort, but it can have a significant impact on personal and professional success. By practicing self-awareness, empathy, and communication skills, individuals can better manage their emotions, build stronger relationships, and become more resilient in the face of challenges.

Chapter 10

IMPROVING COMMUNICATION

Effective communication is an essential component of building and maintaining relationships, both personal and professional. It is the process of exchanging information, thoughts, and feelings between two or more individuals. Communication is vital because it enables people to understand and connect with one another, to build trust and respect, to share ideas and feelings, and to collaborate effectively.

Communication involves a variety of skills, including listening, speaking, nonverbal communication, and writing. Each of these skills is important in its own right and plays a unique role in the communication process. Listening is the ability to hear and understand what others are saying, while speaking is the ability to articulate your own thoughts and ideas clearly and effectively. Nonverbal communication includes body language, facial expressions, and tone of voice, which can convey emotions and attitudes. Writing involves the ability to express ideas and thoughts clearly and succinctly.

The importance of communication cannot be overstated. It is critical in all aspects of life, from personal relationships to professional interactions. In personal relationships, effective communication allows individuals to build strong connections with others, to express their needs and wants, and to resolve conflicts in a healthy and constructive manner. In professional settings, good communication skills are essential for successful teamwork, for managing relationships with clients and customers, and for building trust and rapport with colleagues.

However, despite the importance of communication, many people struggle with this skill. There are a variety of reasons why communication can be difficult, including fear of rejection or judgment, lack of confidence or skill, and misunderstandings or misinterpretations.

In order to improve communication, it is important to focus on developing specific skills and strategies. Here are some techniques to improve communication:

Active Listening: Active listening involves fully concentrating on what the other person is saying, asking questions for clarification, and reflecting back on what has been said. This helps to ensure that you have understood the message accurately, and also shows that you are fully engaged in the conversation.

Use "I" Statements: When expressing your thoughts and feelings, it can be helpful to use "I" statements rather than "you" statements. For example, saying "I feel frustrated when you interrupt me" is more effective than "You always interrupt me."

Be Clear and Concise: Effective communication requires clarity and conciseness. Be direct and to the point, and avoid rambling or using excessive detail.

Be Mindful of Nonverbal Cues: Nonverbal cues such as body language and tone of voice can convey emotions and attitudes. Be mindful of your own nonverbal cues, and also pay attention to the nonverbal cues of others.

Practice Empathy: Empathy involves putting yourself in the other person's shoes and understanding their perspective. It can be helpful to ask questions and listen actively in order to better understand the other person's thoughts and feelings.

Improving communication skills can have a range of benefits. It can lead to better relationships, more successful collaborations, and increased job satisfaction. Effective communication can also reduce misunderstandings and conflict, leading to more positive and productive interactions.

Strategies to improve communication skills

Effective communication is essential for building strong relationships and achieving personal and professional success. Whether you are communicating with a friend, colleague, or family member, the way you convey your message can determine the outcome of the interaction. In this chapter, we will discuss the importance of communication and provide strategies to improve your communication skills.

The Importance of Communication

Communication is the process of exchanging information, thoughts, and feelings between individuals or groups. Effective communication involves being able to express oneself clearly and listen actively to others. Poor communication can lead to misunderstandings, conflict, and failed relationships. Here are some reasons why communication is important:

Building relationships: Communication is the foundation of all relationships. Whether it is personal or professional, good communication skills are essential for building trust and understanding between individuals.

Resolving conflicts: Conflicts are bound to arise in any relationship. Effective communication skills can help in resolving conflicts amicably and prevent them from escalating.

Achieving success: Effective communication is vital for achieving success in any field. In the workplace, good communication skills can lead to better collaboration, increased productivity, and improved teamwork.

Personal development: Good communication skills can help in personal growth and development. By learning how to express oneself clearly and listen actively, one can gain self-confidence and develop stronger relationships.

Strategies to Improve Communication Skills

Here are some strategies to improve your communication skills:

Listen actively: Active listening involves fully concentrating on the speaker and understanding their message. To become a better listener, focus on the speaker, maintain eye contact, and avoid distractions.

Use clear language: Use clear and concise language when communicating. Avoid using jargon, slang, or overly complicated words that can confuse the listener.

Ask questions: Ask questions to clarify any misunderstandings or to gain more information. This shows that you are interested in what the speaker is saying and helps to avoid misunderstandings.

Be aware of your body language: Your body language can convey a lot about your emotions and intentions. Be aware of your posture, gestures, and facial expressions, and ensure that they are consistent with your message.

Practice empathy: Empathy is the ability to understand and share the feelings of others. When communicating with others, try to put yourself in their shoes and see things from their perspective.

Be respectful: Show respect towards the person you are communicating with. Avoid interrupting, belittling, or dismissing their opinions or ideas.

Use positive language: Use positive language to convey your message. Avoid negative language that can come across as accusatory or judgmental.

Practice assertiveness: Assertiveness involves expressing oneself confidently and respectfully. Practice asserting your opinions and ideas in a clear and concise manner.

Seek feedback: Seek feedback from others to improve your communication skills. Ask for honest feedback on your strengths and weaknesses and work on improving them.

Practice, practice, practice: Like any skill, communication requires practice. Take every opportunity to practice your communication skills, whether it is through casual conversations, public speaking, or group discussions.

By incorporating these strategies into your daily life, you can improve your communication skills and become a better communicator. Remember that effective communication is a two-way process that requires both speaking and listening skills. By actively listening and expressing yourself clearly, you can build stronger relationships, avoid misunderstandings, and achieve personal and professional success.

The importance of active listening

Active listening is an essential communication skill that allows people to understand and connect with others. It involves fully concentrating on the speaker, understanding their perspective, and responding appropriately to the message they are trying to convey. Active listening goes beyond just hearing the words someone is saying; it also involves paying attention to non-verbal cues, such as body language and tone of voice.

Active listening is crucial in personal and professional relationships. It can help people build trust, strengthen relationships, and avoid misunderstandings. When people feel heard and understood, they are more likely to open up and share their thoughts and feelings.

One of the main reasons active listening is so important is because it allows people to gain a deeper understanding of others. By fully concentrating on what someone is saying, people can grasp their perspective and appreciate their point of view. This understanding can help improve relationships, reduce conflict, and enhance collaboration.

Another benefit of active listening is that it encourages people to be more present in the moment. When people are fully engaged in a conversation, they are less likely to be distracted by their own thoughts or outside distractions. This presence can help improve communication and build stronger connections with others.

Active listening can also help people avoid misunderstandings. By clarifying what someone is saying and asking questions to gain a deeper understanding, people can avoid assumptions and misinterpretations. This can prevent conflicts and misunderstandings, leading to more productive and positive interactions.

Furthermore, active listening can help people develop empathy and emotional intelligence. By understanding another person's perspective and acknowledging their feelings, people can build stronger emotional connections and develop a greater sense of compassion.

Active listening is a vital communication skill that can benefit personal and professional relationships in many ways. By fully concentrating on the speaker, understanding their perspective, and responding appropriately to the message they are trying to convey, people can build trust, strengthen relationships, avoid misunderstandings, and improve emotional intelligence.

Chapter 11

MANAGING STRESS

S tress is a natural physical and mental response to a perceived threat or demand. It can be experienced in various forms, including emotional, psychological, and physiological. Stress is a natural part of life, and in some situations, it can be beneficial, such as when it motivates us to take action or respond to a challenge. However, excessive stress or chronic stress can have negative impacts on our health, relationships, and overall well-being.

When the body senses a threat, the sympathetic nervous system is activated, and a complex chain reaction begins. This response is known as the "fight or flight" response and triggers the release of adrenaline and cortisol hormones. Adrenaline increases heart rate and blood pressure, while cortisol releases glucose to provide the body with an energy boost to help respond to the perceived threat.

While short-term stress can be helpful, chronic stress can lead to physical and emotional health problems. Prolonged exposure to stress can weaken the immune system, increase the risk of heart disease, and cause anxiety and depression.

There are various types of stress, including acute stress, episodic acute stress, and chronic stress. Acute stress is a short-term stress response, such as a job interview or public speaking, which typically resolves itself once the situation has passed. Episodic acute stress is a pattern of repeated acute stress responses, often experienced by people with a chaotic lifestyle or who are constantly under pressure. Chronic stress, on the other hand, is prolonged stress that continues over an extended period, such as long-term financial or work-related stress.

Stress can be caused by various factors, including personal, work-related, and environmental factors. Personal factors may include relationship problems, financial difficulties, or health concerns, while work-related factors may include excessive workload, conflict with colleagues, or job insecurity. Environmental factors may include natural disasters, pollution, or noise pollution.

It is essential to manage stress to maintain good physical and mental health. By managing stress, individuals can improve their overall quality of life and reduce the risk of health problems. There are various techniques for managing stress, including exercise, relaxation techniques, mindfulness, and seeking social support. It is also important to identify the causes of stress and work on strategies to reduce or manage them.

Stress is a natural response to perceived threats, and while it can be beneficial in some situations, chronic stress can lead to negative health outcomes. Understanding the causes and types of stress is an important step towards managing it effectively.

The different types of stress

Stress is an inevitable part of life that affects us all in one way or another. It can be defined as the body's response to a perceived threat, challenge, or change in our environment. While some level of stress can be beneficial and motivate us to take action, chronic or excessive stress can have negative effects on our physical and mental health.

There are several different types of stress that individuals may experience, including:

Acute stress: This is a type of short-term stress that occurs in response to a specific situation or event. Examples of acute stress include getting into an argument with someone, narrowly avoiding an accident, or receiving a sudden piece of bad news.

Episodic acute stress: This type of stress occurs when an individual experiences acute stress on a regular basis. People who suffer from anxiety, worry, or who tend to catastrophize are more likely to experience episodic acute stress.

Chronic stress: This type of stress occurs when an individual experiences ongoing stressors that they perceive as out of their control. Examples of chronic stress include financial troubles, a difficult job or work environment, or an ongoing health condition.

Traumatic stress: This type of stress is caused by exposure to a traumatic event, such as a natural disaster, serious accident, or violent crime.

Developmental stress: This type of stress is associated with life transitions and changes, such as marriage, divorce, parenthood, or retirement.

Environmental stress: This type of stress is caused by factors in an individual's environment, such as noise, air pollution, or overstimulation.

It is important to note that individuals may experience multiple types of stress at the same time, and the effects of stress can accumulate over time if not properly managed.

Regardless of the type of stress, prolonged or chronic exposure to stress can have negative effects on both physical and mental health. Chronic stress has been linked to a wide range of health problems, including heart disease, high blood pressure, weakened immune function, digestive issues, and mental health conditions such as anxiety and depression. Additionally, stress can impact our daily lives, leading to decreased productivity, poor decision-making, and strained relationships.

Managing stress effectively is therefore essential to promoting overall health and well-being. This may involve identifying sources of stress, learning stress-management techniques, and adopting lifestyle habits that promote resilience and stress reduction.

Acute stress: This type of stress is the most common and is a normal response to a specific event or situation, such as a deadline or public speaking. Acute stress usually resolves quickly and doesn't have long-term effects on health.

Chronic stress: This type of stress is ongoing and lasts for an extended period of time, such as months or even years. Chronic stress can have serious negative effects on physical and mental health, including increased risk for heart disease, depression, and anxiety disorders.

Eustress: This type of stress is often referred to as "positive stress" and can be a motivating force for achievement and growth. Examples of eustress include the excitement of a new job or starting a new relationship.

Distress: This type of stress is often referred to as "negative stress" and is associated with negative emotions, such as anxiety, anger, and sadness. Distress can be caused by a variety of factors, such as a traumatic event, financial difficulties, or relationship problems.

Additionally, it could be useful to discuss the physiological and psychological responses to stress, such as the release of stress hormones like cortisol and adrenaline, increased heart rate and blood pressure, and the fight-or-flight response.

Techniques to manage stress

Stress is an inevitable part of life, and it can have both positive and negative effects on our mental and physical health. While some stress can be beneficial in motivating us to achieve our goals, prolonged exposure to stress can lead to various health problems, such as anxiety, depression, and heart disease. Therefore, it is essential to learn effective techniques to manage stress and prevent it from becoming chronic. In this chapter, we will explore different strategies to manage stress.

Identify and eliminate stressors

The first step in managing stress is to identify the sources of stress in your life. These could be work-related, financial, relationship problems, or health issues. Once you have identified your stressors, try to eliminate or reduce them as much as possible. For example, if you find that your job is causing you significant stress, you may need to consider changing jobs or finding ways to reduce your workload.

Practice relaxation techniques

Relaxation techniques, such as deep breathing, meditation, and yoga, are effective ways to reduce stress levels. These techniques help to calm the mind and body and promote feelings of relaxation and well-being. Deep breathing involves taking long, slow breaths, filling your lungs with air, and exhaling slowly. Meditation involves focusing your mind on a particular object or thought, and yoga involves performing specific poses and breathing exercises.

Exercise regularly

Exercise is an excellent way to manage stress. It helps to reduce tension in the body and release endorphins, which are natural mood-boosting chemicals. Regular exercise can also help to improve your sleep, which is essential for managing stress.

Practice time management

Poor time management can lead to stress and anxiety, as you may feel overwhelmed by your workload and struggle to keep up with deadlines. Learning effective time management skills can help you to prioritize your tasks and reduce your stress levels. Make a to-do list and allocate specific times for completing each task. Avoid multitasking, as this can increase stress levels and reduce productivity.

Seek social support

Social support is a vital tool for managing stress. Talking to someone about your problems can help you to gain a different perspective and develop coping strategies. Friends, family members, or a therapist can provide emotional support and guidance.

Get adequate sleep

Sleep is essential for managing stress. Lack of sleep can make you more vulnerable to stress and anxiety. Ensure that you get enough sleep each night by establishing a regular sleep routine. Try to go to bed and wake up at the same time each day and create a relaxing sleep environment.

Practice self-care

Taking care of you is essential for managing stress. Self-care involves taking steps to improve your physical and mental health, such as eating a healthy diet, getting regular exercise, practicing relaxation techniques, and engaging in activities that you enjoy.

Avoid unhealthy coping mechanisms

Many people turn to unhealthy coping mechanisms, such as alcohol or drug use, to deal with stress. These behaviors may provide temporary relief, but they can lead to more significant problems in the long run. It is essential to find healthy ways to manage stress.

Stress is an inevitable part of life, but it is possible to manage it effectively. By identifying your stressors and practicing relaxation techniques, regular exercise, time management, seeking social support, getting adequate sleep, practicing self-care, and avoiding unhealthy coping mechanisms, you can reduce your stress levels and improve your overall well-being.

There are many techniques to manage stress, and it is important to find the ones that work best for each individual. Here are some additional techniques to consider:

Practice Mindfulness: Mindfulness is the practice of being present and fully engaged in the current moment. It can be a powerful tool for managing stress, as it helps to reduce the negative impact of stress on the mind and body. Mindfulness techniques can include meditation, deep breathing exercises, and body scanning.

Practice Gratitude: Focusing on the positive aspects of life and being grateful for what we have can help to shift our perspective and reduce stress. Keeping a gratitude journal, listing three things we are grateful for each day, or simply taking a moment to appreciate the good things in our lives can all be effective ways to cultivate gratitude.

Exercise: Physical activity can be a powerful stress reliever. It releases endorphins, which are the body's natural mood boosters, and can help to reduce anxiety and depression. Exercise can include activities such as walking, jogging, yoga, or weightlifting.

Get Enough Sleep: Getting enough sleep is essential for managing stress. Lack of sleep can lead to irritability, fatigue, and difficulty concentrating, which can all exacerbate stress. Establishing a regular sleep routine, avoiding caffeine and alcohol before bed, and creating a relaxing sleep environment can all help to improve sleep quality.

Set Boundaries: Learning to say "no" and establishing boundaries can help to reduce stress levels. This can include setting limits on work hours, saying no to activities or commitments that are not essential, and taking time for self-care activities.

Connect with Others: Social support is essential for managing stress. Connecting with friends and family, joining a support group, or participating in a hobby or activity can all help to reduce stress and promote well-being.

Practice Self-Care: Taking care of ourselves is essential for managing stress. This can include engaging in activities that we enjoy, such as reading, taking a bath, or practicing a hobby, as well as taking care of our physical health by eating a healthy diet and staying hydrated.

Seek Professional Help: If stress becomes overwhelming or interferes with daily life, it may be necessary to seek professional help. This can include therapy, counseling, or medication, and can be a helpful tool for managing stress and promoting well-being.

Practice relaxation techniques: Activities like yoga, meditation, deep breathing, and progressive muscle relaxation can help you relax and reduce stress.

Get enough sleep: Lack of sleep can increase stress levels. Aim for 7-9 hours of sleep per night.

Engage in physical activity: Exercise releases endorphins, which are natural mood boosters. Engaging in regular physical activity can help reduce stress levels.

Practice time management: Poor time management can lead to feeling overwhelmed and stressed. Prioritize tasks and schedule time for important activities.

Connect with others: Spending time with friends and family can help reduce stress levels. Talking to others about what's bothering you can also help you find solutions and feel better.

Practice mindfulness: Mindfulness involves being present in the moment and paying attention to your thoughts and feelings without judgment. Mindfulness practices, like meditation and deep breathing, can help reduce stress.

Take breaks: Taking breaks throughout the day can help reduce stress and improve productivity. Take short breaks to stretch, walk, or do something enjoyable.

Seek support: If stress is impacting your mental health or overall well-being, consider seeking support from a mental health professional or counselor. They can help you develop coping strategies and manage stress more effectively.

Chapter 12

CULTIVATING SELF-LOVE

Self-love is the practice of caring for oneself, accepting oneself as is, and being kind and compassionate towards oneself. It is important for one's overall well-being and mental health. When individuals cultivate self-love, they are able to establish a healthy relationship with themselves and others around them. Self-love is crucial in achieving personal growth, managing emotions, and building resilience. In this chapter, we will explore the importance of cultivating self-love and how to practice it.

Firstly, self-love helps individuals to develop a positive self-image. When individuals practice self-love, they learn to appreciate their own unique qualities and strengths, and accept their flaws and weaknesses without judgment. This positive self-image leads to a greater sense of self-worth and self-esteem, which in turn helps to build confidence and resilience. With greater confidence, individuals are more likely to take on challenges and opportunities, and be more resilient when faced with setbacks.

Additionally, self-love allows individuals to establish healthy boundaries and engage in self-care. When individuals practice self-love, they learn to recognize their own needs and prioritize their well-being. This involves setting boundaries with others and engaging in activities that bring them joy and relaxation. By taking care of their own needs, individuals are better able to care for others and establish healthy relationships with those around them.

Self-love also plays a role in managing emotions and mental health. When individuals practice self-love, they are able to manage their emotions in a healthy way, rather than suppressing or denying them. They learn to acknowledge their emotions and respond to them with kindness and compassion, rather than judgment or criticism. This leads to greater emotional regulation and mental well-being. Now that we understand the importance of self-love, let us explore some ways to cultivate it.

One way to cultivate self-love is to practice self-compassion. Self-compassion involves treating oneself with kindness and understanding, particularly during times of difficulty or stress. It involves recognizing that everyone makes mistakes and experiences challenges, and responding to oneself with the same kindness and support one would offer to a friend. To practice self-compassion, individuals can engage in self-soothing activities such as taking a warm bath, reading a book, or engaging in meditation.

Another way to cultivate self-love is to engage in positive self-talk. Positive self-talk involves speaking to oneself in a kind and supportive manner. It involves replacing negative self-talk with positive affirmations, such as "I am enough" or "I am worthy of love and respect." To practice positive self-talk, individuals can create a list of affirmations and repeat them to themselves regularly.

It is also important to engage in self-care activities to cultivate self-love. Self-care involves engaging in activities that bring joy and relaxation, such as spending time with loved ones, engaging in a hobby, or practicing mindfulness. By taking care of one's physical, emotional, and mental health, individuals can cultivate self-love and establish healthy habits.

In addition, it is important to set healthy boundaries to cultivate self-love. Healthy boundaries involve recognizing one's own needs and communicating them to others in a respectful and assertive manner. It involves saying "no" when necessary and establishing clear expectations with others. By setting healthy boundaries, individuals can establish a greater sense of self-worth and self-respect.

Finally, it is important to practice forgiveness to cultivate self-love. Forgiveness involves letting go of past hurts and resentments, and accepting oneself as is. It involves recognizing that everyone makes mistakes and allowing oneself to move forward without judgment or criticism. To practice forgiveness, individuals can engage in forgiveness exercises such as writing a letter of forgiveness to oneself or others.

Self-love is crucial for a healthy and fulfilling life. It means treating ourselves with kindness, respect, and compassion, as we would treat someone we love. It is a vital aspect of our mental and emotional wellbeing, and it can have a significant impact on our physical health as well.

When we love ourselves, we are better able to recognize our own worth and value. We can acknowledge our strengths and weaknesses without judgment, and we can accept ourselves for who we are. This self-acceptance is an essential foundation for personal growth and development. When we love ourselves, we are more likely to take care of ourselves and make choices that support our health and wellbeing. We are also more likely to set healthy boundaries and avoid negative self-talk or destructive behaviors.

On the other hand, when we lack self-love, we may struggle with feelings of inadequacy or self-doubt. We may engage in self-sabotaging behaviors, such as overeating, substance abuse, or other harmful habits. We may also have difficulty forming healthy relationships, as we may not believe we are deserving of love and respect. In extreme cases, a lack of self-love can lead to mental health issues such as depression, anxiety, and low self-esteem.

Overall, cultivating self-love is essential for a happy and healthy life. It allows us to connect with ourselves on a deeper level, form meaningful relationships with others, and achieve our goals and dreams.

Techniques to cultivate self-love

Self-love is a fundamental aspect of overall well-being and personal growth. It involves the practice of accepting and appreciating oneself for who they are, with all their strengths and weaknesses. When individuals cultivate self-love, they develop a positive relationship with themselves, which can help them to improve their self-esteem, confidence, and emotional well-being. Moreover, self-love is crucial for individuals to form healthy relationships with others as they are better able to understand their own needs and boundaries.

However, self-love is not always easy to achieve, especially for individuals who have experienced trauma, low self-esteem, or mental health issues. It requires intentional effort and practice to develop and maintain. Fortunately, there are numerous techniques that individuals can use to cultivate self-love.

Techniques to cultivate self-love

Practice Self-Care: Practicing self-care is an essential technique for cultivating self-love. This involves engaging in activities that promote physical, emotional, and mental well-being, such as exercise, healthy eating, meditation, and spending time with loved ones. By prioritizing self-care, individuals can develop a stronger connection with themselves and recognize their own needs.

Challenge Negative Self-Talk: Negative self-talk can be detrimental to an individual's self-esteem and overall well-being. To cultivate self-love, individuals must learn to challenge their negative self-talk and replace it with positive affirmations. One technique is to write down negative thoughts and then reframe them into positive affirmations. For instance, "I am not good enough" can be reframed into "I am worthy of love and respect."

Practice Gratitude: Practicing gratitude is a powerful technique for cultivating self-love. It involves focusing on the positive aspects of life and appreciating the present moment. By practicing gratitude, individuals can develop a more positive outlook on life and improve their self-esteem. One technique is to write down three things that you are grateful for every day.

Set Boundaries: Setting boundaries is an essential technique for cultivating self-love. It involves recognizing one's own needs and limits and communicating them to others. By setting boundaries, individuals can prioritize their own well-being and avoid situations that may be harmful or stressful.

Forgive Yourself: Forgiveness is an essential aspect of cultivating self-love. It involves letting go of past mistakes and accepting oneself for who they are. To practice forgiveness, individuals must learn to acknowledge their mistakes, take responsibility for their actions, and let go of guilt and shame. One technique is to write a letter of forgiveness to oneself.

Surround Yourself with Positivity: Surrounding oneself with positivity is a powerful technique for cultivating self-love. It involves spending time with people who uplift and support oneself, as well as engaging in activities that bring joy and fulfillment. By surrounding oneself with positivity, individuals can improve their self-esteem and overall well-being.

Practice Mindfulness: Mindfulness is a powerful technique for cultivating self-love. It involves being present in the moment and accepting oneself without judgment. By practicing mindfulness, individuals can develop a stronger connection with themselves and improve their emotional well-being. One technique is to practice mindful breathing or body scans.

Seek Professional Help: Seeking professional help is an essential technique for cultivating self-love, especially for individuals who have experienced trauma, mental health issues, or low self-esteem. A mental health professional can provide support and guidance in developing self-love and improving overall well-being.

Practicing self-care: Self-care involves taking care of yourself physically, emotionally, and mentally. This can include taking breaks when needed, engaging in activities that bring you joy, getting enough sleep and exercise, and eating a healthy diet.

Challenging negative self-talk: Negative self-talk can be damaging to your self-esteem and overall well-being. To cultivate self-love, it's important to recognize when negative self-talk is happening and challenge those thoughts by replacing them with positive and affirming ones.

Practicing self-compassion: Being kind and understanding towards yourself can go a long way in cultivating self-love. Practicing self-compassion involves treating yourself with the same kindness and understanding you would give to a friend who is going through a difficult time.

Setting healthy boundaries: Setting healthy boundaries is essential for self-love because it shows that you value yourself and your needs. This can include saying "no" to things that don't align with your values or needs, and prioritizing time for self-care and self-love activities.

Practicing forgiveness: Forgiving yourself for past mistakes and shortcomings is an important part of cultivating self-love. Holding onto guilt and shame can be detrimental to your well-being, so practicing forgiveness can help you let go of those negative feelings and move forward with a positive mindset.

Surrounding you with positivity: Surrounding yourself with positive people and influences can help boost your self-love and overall well-being. This can include spending time with supportive friends and family, listening to uplifting music or podcasts, and reading books or watching movies that inspire and motivate you.

Engaging in self-reflection: Self-reflection involves taking the time to examine your thoughts, feelings, and behaviors. This can help you identify areas where you may need to cultivate more self-love and make positive changes to improve your overall well-being.

Benefits of self-love

Self-love is the practice of treating oneself with kindness, compassion, and acceptance. It involves recognizing and valuing one's own worth, being mindful of one's needs and emotions, and taking care of oneself physically, emotionally, and spiritually. When one cultivates self-love, they reap a wide range of benefits that contribute to their overall well-being and happiness. In this article, we will explore the benefits of self-love in detail.

Increased self-esteem Self-love involves accepting and valuing oneself. When one practices self-love, they become more aware of their strengths and abilities. This awareness leads to increased self-esteem, which is essential for achieving personal and professional goals. High self-esteem also leads to better decision-making, increased confidence, and more fulfilling relationships.

Improved mental health Self-love involves being kind and compassionate towards oneself. This kindness and compassion can help one to cope with negative thoughts and emotions, leading to improved mental health. When one practices self-love, they are better able to recognize and challenge negative self-talk, which can lead to anxiety and depression. Self-love also involves taking care of oneself physically, emotionally, and spiritually, which are all essential components of good mental health.

Better physical health Self-love involves taking care of oneself physically. This includes eating a healthy diet, getting enough sleep, and exercising regularly. When one practices self-love in this way, they improve their physical health. Exercise has been shown to reduce the risk of chronic diseases such as heart disease, diabetes, and cancer. A healthy diet can also reduce the risk of these diseases and improve overall well-being.

More fulfilling relationships

When one practices self-love, they become more aware of their needs and emotions. This awareness allows them to communicate their needs to others, leading to more fulfilling relationships. Self-love also involves setting healthy boundaries and not tolerating toxic behavior from others. This leads to more positive and meaningful relationships.

Increased resilience Self-love involves being kind and compassionate towards oneself, even during difficult times. This kindness and compassion help one to cope with challenging situations and bounce back from adversity. When one practices self-love, they become more resilient and better able to handle stress and adversity.

Improved creativity

When one practices self-love, they become more aware of their thoughts and emotions. This awareness allows them to tap into their creativity and express themselves more authentically. Self-love also involves taking risks and being vulnerable, which are essential components of creativity.

Increased productivity

When one practices self-love, they prioritize their needs and take care of themselves. This leads to increased energy and focus, which can improve productivity. Self-love also involves setting goals and boundaries, which can help one to stay on track and achieve more.

More fulfilling life

When one practices self-love, they become more aware of their needs and desires. This awareness allows them to create a life that is fulfilling and meaningful. Self-love also involves setting goals and pursuing one's passions, leading to a more satisfying and purposeful life.

Self-love is essential for overall well-being and happiness. When one practices self-love, they reap a wide range of benefits, including increased self-esteem, improved mental and physical health, more fulfilling relationships, increased resilience, improved creativity and productivity, and a more fulfilling life. It is important to prioritize self-love and make it a part of one's daily life.

Chapter 13

PRACTICING GRATITUDE

Gratitude can be defined as the quality of being thankful or showing appreciation for the good things in life. It is a positive emotion that involves acknowledging and recognizing the good things in one's life, both big and small. Gratitude is not just about saying thank you, but it is also about feeling a sense of appreciation and recognizing the value and meaning of what one has.

Gratitude has been found to have numerous benefits for mental and physical health. It can improve mood, increase happiness and life satisfaction, reduce stress and anxiety, and improve relationships. By practicing gratitude, individuals can shift their focus from what they lack to what they have, and this can lead to a more positive outlook on life.

There are many ways to practice gratitude, such as keeping a gratitude journal, expressing gratitude to others, practicing mindfulness, and reflecting on the good things in life. By incorporating gratitude into one's daily life, individuals can cultivate a greater sense of well-being and happiness.

Benefits of practicing gratitude

Gratitude can be defined as the quality of being thankful and having the readiness to show appreciation for the good things in life. Practicing gratitude involves intentionally focusing on the positive aspects of one's life and recognizing the good things, big or small, that are often taken for granted. Research has shown that there are many benefits of practicing gratitude, ranging from physical to psychological well-being.

One of the key benefits of practicing gratitude is improved mental health. Numerous studies have found that individuals who practice gratitude on a regular basis experience less anxiety and depression, and have higher levels of life satisfaction and happiness. Gratitude helps to shift one's focus away from negative thoughts and emotions, and instead encourages a more positive outlook on life. It also helps to reduce stress and improve overall mental resilience.

In addition to its effects on mental health, practicing gratitude has also been found to have physical health benefits. A study published in the Journal of Personality and Social Psychology found that participants who wrote about things they were grateful for experienced fewer physical symptoms such as headaches and stomachaches, and even reported exercising more often. Practicing gratitude has also been linked to better sleep quality, lower blood pressure, and a stronger immune system.

Practicing gratitude can also improve relationships with others. Expressing gratitude towards others helps to strengthen social connections and fosters a sense of community. It can help to build trust and encourage a positive environment, leading to more satisfying relationships with others.

There are several ways to practice gratitude. One simple method is to keep a gratitude journal, where individuals can write down things they are thankful for each day. This can be as simple as being grateful for a sunny day or a good cup of coffee, or more significant things like a supportive friend or a loving family. Taking time to reflect on and appreciate the good things in life can help individuals to feel more positive and content.

Another way to practice gratitude is through acts of kindness. Doing something nice for someone else and expressing gratitude for their presence in one's life can be a powerful way to cultivate a sense of gratitude. This could be as simple as sending a thank-you note, or taking the time to listen to someone who needs support.

Meditation is another tool that can be used to practice gratitude. Taking a few minutes each day to reflect on things to be thankful for can help individuals to cultivate a sense of gratitude and increase overall well-being. This can be done through guided meditations or simply taking a few deep breaths and focusing on positive thoughts.

In addition to these techniques, practicing gratitude can also be integrated into one's daily routine. For example, making a conscious effort to express gratitude towards loved ones or coworkers can help to foster positive relationships and create a more supportive environment. Finding ways to appreciate the little things in life, such as a beautiful sunset or a warm hug, can help to cultivate a sense of gratitude and improve overall well-being.

Overall, the benefits of practicing gratitude are numerous and far-reaching. Whether it is improving mental and physical health, strengthening relationships with others, or fostering a more positive outlook on life, incorporating gratitude into one's daily routine can have a significant impact on overall well-being.

Techniques to practice gratitude

Practicing gratitude is an effective way to increase positive emotions and improve overall well-being. It involves focusing on the good things in life and expressing gratitude for them. Gratitude can be practiced in many different ways, and it is important to find a method that works best for each individual. In this chapter, we will discuss various techniques that can be used to practice gratitude.

Gratitude journaling

Gratitude journaling involves writing down things that one is grateful for. This can be done daily, weekly, or whenever the individual feels the need to do so. It is important to be specific and detailed when writing in a gratitude journal. Instead of simply writing "I am grateful for my family," one could write "I am grateful for my sister who always makes me laugh."

Gratitude letters

Gratitude letters involve writing a letter to someone expressing gratitude for their positive impact on one's life. This can be done to thank someone for something they did in the past or simply to express appreciation for who they are. The letter can be delivered to the person or kept for personal reflection.

Gratitude jar

A gratitude jar is a jar filled with notes of things one is grateful for. Whenever something good happens, a note is added to the jar. This can be done individually or as a family. At the end of each year or whenever the jar is full, the notes can be read to reflect on all the good things that happened.

Gratitude meditation

Gratitude meditation involves focusing on feelings of gratitude during meditation. This can be done by simply thinking about things one is grateful for or by repeating a gratitude mantra. For example, one could repeat the phrase "I am grateful for this moment" during meditation.

Gratitude walk

A gratitude walk involves taking a walk and focusing on things to be grateful for in the surroundings. This can include the beauty of nature, the kindness of others, or anything else that brings feelings of gratitude.

Gratitude jar of blessings

A gratitude jar of blessings is similar to a gratitude jar but involves focusing on blessings that have not yet happened. This involves writing down something that one hopes for or wants to achieve, expressing gratitude as if it has already happened. For example, one could write "I am grateful for getting the job I applied for."

Gratitude board

A gratitude board involves creating a physical board with pictures, quotes, or other items that represent things one is grateful for. This can be displayed in a prominent place to serve as a visual reminder of all the good things in life.

Gratitude sharing

Gratitude sharing involves expressing gratitude to others verbally. This can be done by thanking someone for something they did or simply telling them how much they mean to you. This can be done in person, over the phone, or even through a handwritten note.

Overall, practicing gratitude can have numerous benefits for mental health and well-being. By focusing on the positive aspects of life and expressing gratitude, individuals can increase their happiness, reduce stress, and improve relationships with others. It is important to find a gratitude practice that works best for each individual and to incorporate it into daily life as much as possible.

Chapter 14

NURTURING RELATIONSHIPS

Relationships are an essential aspect of human life. From family and friends to colleagues and acquaintances, our lives are filled with a variety of relationships. These relationships shape our identity and influence our emotions, behavior, and overall wellbeing. In this article, we will discuss the importance of relationships, the benefits of healthy relationships, and some strategies to improve our relationships.

Why Are Relationships Important?

Relationships are important for a variety of reasons. First, relationships provide a sense of belonging and connectedness. We are social creatures, and our need for social connection is fundamental. Relationships allow us to share experiences, thoughts, and feelings with others, and help us feel supported, understood, and validated.

Second, relationships can provide us with emotional and practical support. When we face challenges or difficult times, having someone to talk to, to listen, and to support us can help us cope better. Relationships also provide practical help, such as sharing resources or providing assistance when we need it.

Third, relationships can help us learn and grow. Relationships allow us to share perspectives, learn new things, and gain new insights. Our interactions with others can help us develop new skills, expand our knowledge, and broaden our horizons.

Fourth, relationships are important for our mental and physical health. Research has shown that social support can reduce stress, improve mood, and enhance overall wellbeing. Having supportive relationships can also help us cope better with chronic health conditions and reduce the risk of premature death.

Benefits of Healthy Relationships

Healthy relationships have numerous benefits for our wellbeing. Some of the key benefits are discussed below:

Improved mental health: Healthy relationships can improve our mental health by reducing stress, increasing happiness, and improving our sense of self-worth. A strong support system can help us cope with difficult situations, provide emotional stability, and reduce the risk of depression and anxiety.

Better physical health: Research has shown that people with strong social support have better physical health outcomes, including lower blood pressure, stronger immune systems, and reduced risk of chronic diseases such as heart disease and diabetes.

Increased life satisfaction: Healthy relationships can enhance our overall sense of satisfaction with life. Sharing experiences and creating memories with loved ones can create a sense of purpose and fulfillment.

Improved communication skills: Healthy relationships provide opportunities to practice effective communication, which can improve our ability to express ourselves and understand others.

Strategies to Improve Relationships

While relationships are essential for our wellbeing, they are not always easy to navigate. Relationships can be complex, and conflicts and misunderstandings can arise. However, there are several strategies that can help us improve our relationships and maintain healthy connections with others:

Communication: Effective communication is critical for healthy relationships. It is important to listen actively, express ourselves clearly, and be respectful of others' opinions and feelings.

Boundaries: Establishing and maintaining healthy boundaries is important for maintaining healthy relationships. Boundaries help us communicate our needs and expectations and help us avoid situations that may be harmful or uncomfortable.

Empathy: Practicing empathy involves putting ourselves in someone else's shoes and trying to understand their perspective.

Empathy helps us build connections with others, strengthen relationships, and resolve conflicts.

Forgiveness: Forgiveness is essential for healthy relationships. Holding onto grudges and resentments can damage relationships and cause emotional distress. Forgiveness involves letting go of negative feelings and moving forward with a positive mindset.

Quality time: Spending quality time with loved ones is essential for maintaining healthy relationships. This can involve engaging in shared activities, having meaningful conversations, or simply being present with each other.

Chapter 15

CONCLUSION

C hapter 1 of this book covered the importance of self-awareness and the various factors that can contribute to personal growth. It discussed the need to identify one's strengths, weaknesses, values, and beliefs to better understand oneself and move towards a fulfilling life. Chapter 2 explored the concept of self-care, including physical, mental, and emotional health. It emphasized the importance of taking care of oneself to better handle life's challenges and achieve personal growth.

Chapter 3 focused on mindfulness and its role in personal growth. Mindfulness allows individuals to be present in the moment, non-judgmentally, and develop a greater awareness of themselves and their surroundings. Chapter 4 delved into the topic of inner strength, discussing the different types of inner strength and their importance in building resilience and overcoming self-doubt.

Chapter 5 explored the topic of change, acknowledging the difficulties that come with it and providing strategies to embrace change. Chapter 6 covered the importance of goal setting and provided guidance on how to set effective goals. Chapter 7 discussed the significance of resilience, defining it as the ability to bounce back from adversity and providing techniques to develop resilience.

Chapter 8 focused on the importance of confidence, discussing the benefits of being confident and strategies to build self-confidence. Chapter 9 delved into the topic of emotional intelligence, defining it as the ability to recognize, understand, and manage one's own emotions and those of others. It provided techniques to enhance emotional intelligence.

Chapter 10 explored the importance of communication and provided strategies to improve communication skills. Chapter 11 focused on the topic of stress, discussing the different types of stress and techniques to manage stress. Chapter 12 covered the importance of self-love and provided techniques to cultivate self-love.

Chapter 13 delved into the topic of gratitude, defining it as the practice of recognizing and appreciating the positive aspects of life. It discussed the benefits of practicing gratitude and provided techniques to practice gratitude. Finally, Chapter 14 explored the importance of relationships and how they contribute to personal growth.

The key points of this book have been to encourage readers to embark on a journey of self-discovery and personal growth. This involves developing self-awareness, practicing self-care, cultivating mindfulness, building inner strength, embracing change, setting effective goals, developing resilience, building confidence, enhancing emotional intelligence, improving communication skills, managing stress, cultivating self-love, and practicing gratitude. The journey towards personal growth is not easy, but it is essential for leading a fulfilling and meaningful life.

As you continue on your journey of self-discovery and personal growth, it is important to remember that growth is a process. It requires patience, perseverance, and dedication. You may encounter setbacks, challenges, and obstacles along the way, but do not let them discourage you. Use them as opportunities to learn, grow, and become stronger. Remember to celebrate your progress, no matter how small it may seem. Finally, surround yourself with supportive people who believe in you and your journey towards personal growth.

Remember that personal growth is a journey, not a destination. Continue to learn, grow, and challenge yourself. Celebrate your progress and surround yourself with positive and supportive people. Remember that you have the power to create the life you want, and with dedication and perseverance, anything is possible.

www.ingramcontent.com/pod-product-compliance
Lightning Source LLC
Chambersburg PA
CBHW071352090426
42738CB00012B/3089